true ghosts

About the Author

Andrew Honigman (Minnesota) has been FATE magazine's Associate Editor since 1999. He has helped hundreds of contributors share their most baffling and extraordinary experiences with FATE's readers.

true ghosts

haunting tales from the vaults of FATE magazine

compiled and edited by

ANDREW HONIGMAN

Llewellyn Publications
Woodbury, Minnesota

First Edition
Second Printing, 2011

Book design by Steffani Sawyer
Cover art: Ghost image © ranplett/iStockphoto and the bare trees image
    © James Lazos/SuperStock
Cover design by Kevin R. Brown
Editing by Ed Day
Llewellyn is a registered trademark of Llewellyn Worldwide Ltd.

Cataloging-in-Publication Data for this title is on file at the Library of Congress.
ISBN: 978-0-7387-1586-5

Llewellyn Publications
A Division of Llewellyn Worldwide Ltd.
2143 Wooddale Drive
Woodbury, Minnesota 55125-2989
www.llewellyn.com

Printed in the United States of America

Other books by Andrew Honigman

True Tales of Ghostly Encounters

Contents

Introduction

Has your life been touched by the supernatural? Chances are good that it has.

Perhaps you have been visited by a spectral apparition or received a message from a long-deceased loved one. You may have lived in a haunted house, or experienced bizarre disruptions of time and space in an energy spot or vortex. Maybe you have even left your physical body to travel the astral plane or glimpse the afterworld. If any of the following is true, you should know you are not alone.

FATE magazine was created in 1948 to document and share just these types of experiences. FATE's founding editors realized almost immediately that their readers would be their best source for reports of unexplained phenomena. Eyewitness accounts of the strange and unknown have been FATE's focus from the very beginning, and readers have been invited to contribute from the start.

I have been FATE's associate editor for the past ten years, and I have been privileged to hear from hundreds of ordinary people trying to make sense out of extraordinary events. The stories collected in this book all date from this period of time. They provide clear evidence that the world in the 21st century is just as weird and wonderful as it has even been.

I hope you enjoy reading these sincere and baffling accounts, and I hope someday you will share your own ghost stories with FATE.

—*Andrew Honigman*

1

Ghostly Apparitions

The classic ghost report, an encounter with a spirit in visible form, may be the easiest to understand and yet the hardest to explain. To see the image of someone known to be deceased, looking much as the person did in life, makes a kind of intuitive sense. How else would a ghost appear? Then again, why should a disembodied spirit take the form of a body it has transcended? By what mechanism does this happen?

The lore of ghost hunters and parapsychologists suggests that some apparitions might be better understood as psychic impressions or environmental recordings. These phantoms do not interact with observers and do not appear conscious of their present surroundings as they endlessly repeat their mindless routines. How and why such an impression or recording comes about is not known, but it is usually associated with an intensely emotional event (such as a battle or murder) or a strong attachment formed in life to a particular location.

Apparitions that interact and communicate with the living seem to represent something of another nature entirely. Sightings of recently deceased loved ones are most common in our files, and tend to support the idea that the human personality survives physical death. Skeptics find such reports easy to explain away as grief-induced hallucinations. However, cases abound of apparitions with multiple witnesses, as well as spirits who provide information that can be indepently verified.

The true nature of ghostly apparitions may never be known, but the intense feelings they inspire, from terror and awe to reassurance and comfort, are undeniably real.

A Visit from My Dad

My entire family pooh-poohed the idea of ghosts, spirits, and supernatural events, especially my daddy. The very thought of those things made him laugh. But it was he who came to see me several years after his death.

I grew up, graduated, went to college, married, and had four beautiful children. Unfortunately, this marriage ended in divorce. In the meantime, my father had died, as had my grandmother, and my mother and grandfather had purchased a smaller home so she could look after him in his declining years.

My husband and I had purchased the old antebellum home in Palestine, Texas, in which I had grown up, shortly before the divorce. I thought that we would retire there. But my husband had other plans—obtaining a younger companion being one of them. In fact, she was the first of many.

Over the months, with growing children, the dissolved marriage, and the struggle to stay on my feet, the thought of ghosts, supernatural sights, and eerie happenings took a back seat to more pressing matters.

I had moved everything out of the front room, where my grandparents had lived, to make room for a ceramic shop I had purchased. The only things left in the room were the massive dining room table and chairs where my family had gathered every Thanksgiving and Christmas, laughing as we shared the love and togetherness that had been our way of life.

One day, I stood in the middle of the room trying to imagine where the counters, shelves, and display tables would be. I heard a chuckle and looked up to see my daddy sitting at the dining room table, looking as natural as could be.

"What'cha doing, honey?" he drawled, smiling that familiar smile of his. He sat leaning slightly over the table with his arms crossed on the surface, a pose I had seen hundreds of times. It was a sight as natural and ordinary as breathing.

"I bought a ceramic shop, Daddy," I answered, without thinking. "I'm trying to decide where to put everything." I pointed toward the large front window. "I'm thinking of putting a table there with the larger pieces that can be seen from the street."

Dadded smiled and nodded. As I turned back toward the window, the truth suddenly dawned on me: Daddy had passed way several years before. I turned quickly around and watched him, still smiling and nodding, fade away. My heart was pounding and my palms were damp—not from fear, but from the thrill and the joy of seeing my daddy again. It never occurred to me to be afraid.

I walked into the hallway and shakily lowered myself onto the second step of the staircase, a silly smile pasted on my face. I was elated.

I hope you are as lucky as I was to have the opportunity to see someone you have lost, and that you are as thrilled as I was when it happens.

—*Bobbie Shafer,*
Troup, Tex.

That's Not Bunny!

Although I may wish to possess the capability, I'll be the first to admit to personally lacking supernatural awareness. There was one event, though, to which I was an indirect party; an occurrence that, given the integrity of those involved and the way in which it happened, leaves little doubt in my mind that something extraordinary transpired.

My family was never given to superstition. My mother was of proper English stock. My father, of German descent, was a practical man who had no time for "otherworldly nonsense." When he resigned his post in the Secret Service at the beginning of 1949, we headed south to a new life in Miami, Florida.

We moved into a plain, two-story apartment building in Coral Gables, a well-kept residential section of the city. Our modest rooms overlooked a quiet street, small courtyard, and a patch of woods.

One evening I lay in bed in a long, plain nightgown. My mother, adamant about her nine-year-old getting proper rest, made certain as usual that I was in my room at an early hour. Not yet sleepy, I sang softly to myself, planning the next day's adventures. I could hear my parents conversing in the nearby living room. There was, of course, no television, only low music drifting in from the kitchen radio. Due to daylight saving time, total darkness was still a few minutes away. Lights were dimmed.

Suddenly I heard my mother exclaim in a scolding tone. "Look! There's Bunny! That little scamp has gotten out of bed when she should be asleep!" ("Bunny" was her nickname for me.)

My attention was immediately riveted. *What is she talking about?* I wondered. *I'm right where I'm supposed to be.*

For a moment there was silence. Then my father answered in a tight voice. "That's not Bunny, that's your mother!"

But my grandmother was dead! I had never even met her! I lay frozen in bed, puzzled, confused; too fearful to speak.

My mother gasped. Their voices fell silent. When they finally spoke it was in whispers.

An eternity later I fell asleep.

The next morning my mother related what they saw. Someone had appeared in the passageway between the living room and the bedrooms. At first, she thought it was me, but my father had instantly recognized the apparition as his mother-in-law, dead for some 20 years. My mother then realized that it was indeed her beloved mother! The spirit, less than 15 feet away, soon faded into nothingness. My parents were left with only questions and bewilderment.

Not one of us had been discussing the supernatural. I was certainly not playing tricks. My parents were definitely not the type to "see ghosts." There were only two doors, both locked and in sight of the couch on which my parents were sitting. No one could have entered into the second-story apartment unnoticed.

Is there an explanation? To this day I wonder.

—*Cynthia Williams Wright,*
Palm City, Fla.

Suburban Diner

Suburban Diner was my friend Sylvester C. Scott's favorite diner at Route 17 South in Paramus, New Jersey. It was the only one he patronized, visiting once a month for over 30 years.

On July 25, 2000, at 7:00 a.m., Scott picked me up from work. On our way home, we passed by the diner.

"Let's have breakfast," I suggested.

"Okay," he said.

The parking lot was empty. Ours was the only car parked at the diner. Bewildered, we looked at each other.

We entered the front door and walked toward the second door that would lead us to the diner's interior. I was ahead of Scott, but before I stepped in, hands still clutching the doorknob, I peeped through and scanned the area.

The dining room was empty, completely devoid of people. Lights were subdued, and I could hardly see. Dining tables and chairs were neatly arranged as if waiting for diners. The counter bar surrounded by high stools was empty of people and food. It was so eerie I almost backed out.

Then I saw an elderly white couple standing outside the counter bar. The woman was in front of the man. She was in her late 80s, short and petite, wearing a white waitress's uniform with a black apron. He was in his early 90s, wearing a tan suit with a clip-on ribbon tie instead of a necktie. The old woman smiled, so we went in.

Scott and I chose our table, followed by the old woman. We ordered breakfast without a menu. We knew what we wanted and how much it would cost.

Silently she took our orders, left, and was back quickly with our food. The old man was not around.

We ate in silence and were in a hurry to leave. After we finished, we waited and waited and waited. After 45 minutes, I told Scott just to leave the money on the table.

On our way home, we didn't discuss anything. I wondered why the old woman was still waitressing at her age.

The following morning we went back to the diner. We saw three cars in the parking lot. There were three young men inside the diner in animated conversation. One of them came to the door and told us the place was not in business anymore.

Two days later, Suburban Diner was demolished. In place of it now is a gas station.

Who were this couple? I believe they were ghosts: the former owners of the diner. To serve patrons one last time was their desire, and they fulfilled it before their beloved diner was demolished into oblivion.

—Herminia C. del Val,
Teaneck, N.J.

I Will See You Again

I had lived in Ohio since 1968 and had not seen my brother during that period. I had almost erased him from my mind. The first six weeks of 1977 brought nothing but vague dreams of him and my home in Alabama. Each morning I had severe headaches and pains in my chest and arms.

I tried furiously to come up with even the most vague interpretation of the dreams, but each attempt brought only frustration.

A few days later, the urge became more demanding. On Thursday, I left work and headed straight to the interstate.

After driving about ten hours, I began experiencing breathing difficulties and my heart pounded as though it would burst. It was almost dark as I pulled into a gas station in a small town near Chattanooga, Tennessee.

I went into the restaurant after splashing cold water on my face at the pump. I sat down and looked for a waitress. I was distracted by an image entering the café. It was my brother, Bobby, whom I was going to visit. Without saying a word he sat down across from me. All he did was sit there and smile. There was a glow on his face that I had never seen. I was uncomfortable to the point that I couldn't wait to leave. A cold chill permeated my body. I paid the tab and headed for the door. Bobby went to the men's room and I waited by the door. After about 20 minutes, I became concerned. He never came out. I checked each stall in the restroom only to find them all empty.

My imagination ran wild. I thought perhaps he had deliberately slipped out. I returned to my car to fill the tank before continuing my journey. I pulled up to the pump. The pain returned stronger than ever. I slumped over the steering wheel. As the station attendant revived me, I felt I had left my body and floated upward. My entire being was loose and free. Then I felt myself re-enter my body.

I got back on the road and tuned the radio to an Anniston station about 100 miles away. The first thing that came over the air rang throughout my entire being. I froze, dripping cold sweat. The announcer continued: "Heflin youth Bobby Brown was pronounced dead early this morning at the scene of a car/truck collision on Routh 78 at the foot of Heflin Mountain." Heflin was another 200 miles.

When I reached the funeral home hours later, I waited another hour before I could see him. After talking with the funeral director, I realized the sharp pain in my heart coincided with the steering column impacting my brother's chest. This explained the unbearable pain that I had experienced the past week.

The following day a seven-mile-long procession headed from the closely knit town to a small church outside the city limits. The service was short. I found myself standing by the grave dropping a handful of dirt on the shining casket.

As I released the dirt, a gentle breeze kissed my cheek and I heard a faint voice saying, "Thanks for lunch. I love you, always remember that." As I returned to my car, I heard the same faint voice calling, "I will see you again."

It has been almost 30 years since the tragic accident without any message from Bobby. On July 9, 2004, my brother Lyle was preparing for vacation in Florida. Prior to leaving, he purchased a disposable Polaroid camera from a local discount house. I was sitting at my computer when I heard him say, "Smile." I was partially turned when he snapped the picture. He pulled it from the camera and headed toward the door. I was pressed by a deadline and ignored the picture. Later that day, I peeled the backing from the picture and saw an amazingly clear print of Bobby sitting there by my side, infatuated with the mechanics of a computer.

— *Charlie R. Brown,*
Deland, Fla.

My Friend Gary

The summer I was 16, I moved to live with my father. Away from my hometown, away from all of my friends, I missed them, especially Gary. He was like a brother, my very best friend. To this very day I can still see him smiling, laughing, and gently chiding me about the hazards of smoking.

One night in late July, I received a phone call from my older sister saying she had bad news for me. Someone had died. My heart skipped, pounded in fearful anticipation.

"Now don't you cry," she said.

But I was already crying. I heard the distress and sympathy in her voice, and I knew I had lost someone close and special to me.

"Gary Piper died," she said. "He had an accident at work."

My mind instantly flashed back to the last day of school, the last time I saw Gary. He ran up to me, panting slightly.

"Hey Lor, have you seen Maggie?"

I smiled into his blue eyes. I knew how much he cared for Maggie. They had been dating for quite some time and he was head over heels for her. It was his first touch of love.

"Sorry, Gary, I haven't seen her."

Before I could tell him I was moving, he took off running down the hall, shouting over his shoulder,

"Thanks anyway, Lor. If you see her, tell her I am looking for her. See ya!"

Such loss and emptiness filled me that night. The tall, skinny, curly-headed youth that I had shared so much with was gone. I hadn't even said goodbye to him. Unable to attend Gary's funeral, I was desolate, heartbroken, hurting. Unable to let go of my friend, of the pain. The hardest part was knowing I had to let go, but not knowing how. How could I when I hadn't even had a chance to say goodbye?

Trying to distract me from my pain, my father asked me if I'd be interested in a job. I knew I needed a diversion, so I agreed, and he set me up with a job mowing the lawn at a local United Baptist Church. It was a sunny, warm day and I didn't mind the physical labor.

Suddenly the hair on the back of my neck tingled. I stopped mowing in puzzlement. I could feel someone staring at me. I looked over my left shoulder, and discovered that I was indeed being stared at. It was Gary! I looked at him standing there watching me. He was wearing blue jeans and a T-shirt. Seconds that felt like years went by as we gazed at each other.

Suddenly I thought, *It can't be Gary, he's dead!* I whipped my head away, instantly turning back again for another look. He was gone. The street was empty. Frantically I looked all around for signs of another person. Whoever it was couldn't have disappeared from sight in a matter of seconds. But he had.

Shortly afterward, another friend from my hometown came to visit me. I told him of my experience, and he looked at me in amazement. He had seen Gary the day he died. I had described perfectly the clothing he was wearing at the time of his accident. I also discovered another amazing thing: Gary was buried in a United Baptist Church cemetery.

This is survival; survival of the soul and of love. Both continue to exist, even in death. Gary proved that to me.

—*Lori LeBlanc-Ault,*
Allen, Tex.

Violet's Visit

My two daughters have always been very psychic, and I have had my share of experiences through the years. But I had always assumed that my two sons, who are both in the military, didn't have psychic ability or interest in the subject.

Several years ago, the girls and I were renting an old farmhouse which had recently been sold by the elderly couple who had lived there for over 50 years. We saw the past owners occasionally since they lived within a few miles of us, but we followed their progress mostly by the gossip so common in a small community.

We heard about the wife, Violet, who was enjoying her new home, and about how hard life had been for her on the farm. Still, she had raised five children there and done the best she could with what she had. Her husband, Oliver, apparently begrudged every dime she spent on the new home and sulked over simple expenses even though the price they got for the farm was in the millions.

It was about a year after the sale of the farm that Violet died. We were sad to think that she had had so little time to enjoy her retirement.

A few days after Violet passed, my youngest son, Dean, arrived from his Marine base for a visit. He had not been to the farmhouse before and consequently knew nothing of the previous owners. A large sofa had been left in the living room by the farm family and he opted to sleep there.

Early next morning, I was cooking breakfast when Dean came in from his run. "So who's the old lady in the apron?" he asked.

Startled, I asked what he was talking about, and he told me he had been awakened in the middle of the night by an elderly woman in a print dress and apron. She was dusting the coffee table and rearranging the books and magazines on it. He described Violet in detail, even though he had never heard about her and certainly had never seen her. I asked what he had done when he saw her, and he said since she wasn't bothering him, he rolled over and went back to sleep. I should add that the room was well lit by a yard light which was quite near the living room window.

If one of the girls had seen Violet, I wouldn't have been so surprised. Having my Marine son tell me about her certainly left no room for doubt that at least once, Violet had returned to her old home to say goodbye.

So far as I know, she has never been seen again.

—*Sylvia Webb-Hutchins,*
Bellingham, Wash.

My Italian Grandfather

My grandfather died in the spring of 1977. Being the oldest grandchild, I was very close to him. For one thing, I was the only grandchild who spoke Italian fluently.

On the night my grandfather died, I made two phone calls to Italy to tell his older sister and nephew about his passing. It was hard to say *mio nonno e' morto.* But respect to the family elders in Italy demanded that it be done.

I went to Italy that summer. This trip, however, was much more than just a pleasurable break from school. It was also to pay respects to my grandfather's older sister, and to make sure she was all right. I knew that my grandfather would have wanted this.

My family in Italy lives in an old town called Gioi Cilento. Most of the buildings date back to the time of Columbus. My family's house is no exception; the date 1520 is clearly inscribed in the massive, clay-colored stone structure. There were stories of spiritual visitations connected with the house, but I gave them no mind—until one morning.

On this particular morning, the sun was shining through the blinds. I remember looking at the alarm clock on top of the night table; it was a little after 8:00. I heard the usual morning din beneath my window— the conversations, the braying of mules, and the roar of tractors going into the fields. Not giving it a second thought, I turned on my back and continued to recline in bed. That's when it happened.

Suddenly I got this feeling of dread. I began having cold sweats and shivering. I found that no matter how hard I tried, I couldn't move a single muscle. I was only able to grunt, groan, and whimper in fear. Then things got even more frightful! I still get goosebumps thinking about it.

Entering the room through the door was a specter. I quickly recognized this apparition to be my grandfather. He was wearing the same black suit we buried him in that spring. He glided effortlessly through the door and approached me. Once he got near me, he smiled and kissed me on the forehead. Then, as if awakening from a dream, the apparition vanished, leaving me quivering in fear. The whole episode lasted for only a few minutes.

I do not know what triggered the event. I would like to think that it was Grandpa telling me that everything was all right. However, whatever happened on that summer morning in 1977 totally changed my perspective on parapsychology and the hereafter.

—*John Di Genio,*
South Korea

Visit from My Dad

My dad passed away in 1991 and we have had many visits from him in many different ways. The most recent happened in June 2005. A friend of mine, Mike Belair, was in a car accident. I asked him to stay at my home with my daughter and I while he recovered from his injuries.

Mike had injured his leg and was required to wear a leg brace. I asked my mother if he could borrow one of Dad's canes to help him get around. My mother brought three of Dad's canes for Mike to choose from. The one that worked the best was the same cane that Dad used most of the time. Mike took the cane into his bedroom that night.

The next morning, Mike asked me the most peculiar question. He wanted to know if I had come into his room in the night and had taken his boxer shorts off and pulled all the covers off of him. I laughed at the question, but he was quite serious. He said his boxers were neatly folded in thirds at the end of the bed. He also said that when he was trying to sleep, he rolled over and thought he saw a man in a suit standing by the bed.

I asked if the man was slim and short. Mike said yes, he was. He said he rolled over because he thought he was seeing things. I knew instantly it was my dad. I called my mother to ask how Dad folded his underwear, and sure enough, it was in thirds.

Dad had a really wild sense of humor, so I could understand the underwear ending up where they did. I told Mike he had a visit from Dad.

Mike continued to use Dad's cane that day, and in the evening we decided to watch a movie. We had our chairs lined up in front of the television and were watching a war movie when the strong smell of cherry pipe tobacco came into the room. Dad smoked a pipe and used cherry tobacco. It started with my daughter, moved to me, and then settled over Mike. All the hair on the back of his neck stood up and you could feel a cold spot that settled over on top of him.

This really freaked us all out. The cane stayed in the living room when we went to bed and nothing happened that night.

The next day, we returned the cane to my mother and that was the last time Dad came to visit. I guess he came along with his cane and went back home with it.

—*Karen Oswald,*
Lambertville, Mich.

Someone To Watch Over Me

Some people are more open to mystic experiences than others, and I believe there are also locations that are more receptive as well. In the early 1990s, I lived in a tiny town in upstate New York. Chaumont is located near Lake Ontario and it thrives on the hunting and fishing sector of the tourism industry. Our home was built in the late 1800s.

Unfortunately, the relationship between my boyfriend and I was becoming strained. I started struggling with a decision about whether or not to return to Texas. One morning I woke up, squinting from the sunlight that was streaming through the windows. I was on my side facing the closet. As soon as my eyes opened, I saw three figures standing in front of me: a tall man, a woman, and a stout man.

I rolled over and exclaimed to Jim, "There are three people standing next to the bed!"

Jim sat up, looked around, and then he said, "You're dreaming."

I was definitely not dreaming. My heart was pounding, and I was so certain those people were still there that I was afraid to look. I stayed like that with my back to the closet for several minutes, trying to muster the resolve to roll over. When I finally felt it was safe to look, they were gone.

Later that day I phoned my mother and told her about the experience. She asked me to describe the people. When I finished, she immediately said the tall man was her boyfriend, the woman was my aunt, and the other man was a close friend of our family. All three had died within the previous few years. Mom was positive that those people, who had cared about me in life, were watching over me and had come to offer me comfort.

When your life is in turmoil, you frequently look for signs that things will improve. It's often when you aren't looking that something special happens.

—*Leslie Kay Radice,*
McKinney, Tex.

An Unexpected Visit

Upon the moment of my father's death in 1964, his spirit visited me. He'd lived in our hometown of Louisville, Kentucky, with his mother. I was living with my husband and three young children in Chagrin Falls, Ohio. The only time I was able to return to Louisville had been when my mother died, as money was scarce, and Daddy, a chronic alcoholic, had no means to travel.

It was about 11:00 on a September Saturday night. Our children were fast asleep. I was just nodding off but awoke abruptly, screaming hysterically and bawling my eyes out. My husband grabbed his flashlight and leapt out of bed, fearing an intruder had broken in. Our three startled children came darting into the room. For about an hour (it seemed like forever to me) I could neither be reached nor comforted, my eyes glazed over with what my son later described as "a thousand-yard stare."

All during my dad's spirit visitation, my childhood memories were flashing before my eyes. I could see, hear, and feel my dad's newly liberated soul tugging and pulling at me, actively urging me to go with him into the Light. Finally, and this I recall most vividly, an indescribable sense of peace enveloped me. My tears ceased to flow, and I said confidently "I know what's wrong. My daddy's dead."

He'd tried to get me to cross over with him, telling me: "It's so beautiful over here!"

I never doubted that he'd always loved me, but his emotional torment in life had been too great for such endearing assurances ever to be uttered, not even once. And though I surely wanted to go with him into the Light, I had to refuse. I could not leave my children, certainly not like that.

Early Sunday morning I tried to phone him at Grandma's house. Grandma had died just two weeks prior. I knew there'd be no answer on the other end of the line, but I needed to find out if he'd actually passed away—was it all a dream? Sure enough, his sister called a few hours later to inform me that he had in fact died the night before while sitting comfortably in his kitchen rocker. Apparently he'd spent his last earthly hours sober, with a cup of coffee sitting beside him. Many years later, I discovered that he'd deliberately ended his own life by swallowing a bottle of sleeping pills. He'd worked as an artist and painter, and was always kind to everyone. But his depressive alcoholism had scarred our lives forever.

Looking back over the years, through the ineffable screen of my life's experience, I've learned, at least in my daddy's case, that alcoholism is an insidious form of escapism, as is probably true of drug addiction, obsessive meditation, or any other chronic dependency that tends to alienate its habitués from the outside world—too often at the expense of their family, friends, livelihood, health, and eventually their life.

Subsequent to my father's death and visitation more than four decades ago, I have experienced additional visitations from the other side. There can be no question that soul is immortal. And that's good news for everyone, no matter what their beliefs may be.

—*Carolyn Mingus,*
Evergreen, Colo.

Cross in the Ditch

I would like to share an experience that happened to me, my brother Brian, and his wife Mary.

Although I can't recall the exact date or year, I do know that it was a frosty October night in the late

1980s. We all rode together in my brother's truck to work at Ashley Furniture in Arcadia, Wisconsin. It was a 50-mile drive each way from Augusta, where we lived, along back country roads loaded with deer, farms, and a couple small towns.

We worked the swing shift, and one night we were on our way home at about 2:00 in the morning. It was the home stretch between Osseo and Augusta on County Road R. There was heavy fog in some areas, and it was perfectly clear in others. I remember telling my brother to slow down and watch for deer. Then, just ahead in a clear area, we saw an older man dressed in a white suit, white hat, white beard, and an old-style tie. He looked sort of like the Kentucky Fried Chicken guy, and had an old suitcase covered with stickers like you sometimes see from the older days.

As we went past, I made eye contact with the old man and saw that he was in distress. I asked my brother to stop and at least offer him a ride in the back of the truck. Brian stopped and started to back up. I watched to make sure we didn't run over the old man, but I couldn't see him. He had disappeared. There was nowhere he could have gone to that quickly. The corn-fields were already harvested on both sides of the road.

When I looked down along the ditch, I saw a white cross that had been overgrown with tall weeds. I told Brian that was where the old man was standing. He spun his tires and took off out of there. No one said anything the rest of the way home.

We drove past that area every day, but we never saw him again. I always got goosebumps and tried to avoid looking at the cross in the ditch whenever we passed it.

—*Dan Dehnke,*
Blaine, Wash.

Spirit of Love

My husband's illness had reached a point where only time would tell how long he would remain with the family. A massive stroke had paralyzed the left side of his body, only increasing complications to his already failing health. An intense, three-month stay in the hospital didn't produce much hope. He had to be sent to a nursing home for specialized therapy that I hoped would produce an improvement.

I was at the hospital when he slipped into a diabetic coma; one that couldn't be reversed. By mid-afternoon, it became apparent that the end was nearing.

The children were called; three of four were able to be there to say their goodbyes. The fourth lived 1,500 miles away and called periodically throughout the rest of the day.

My daughter stayed as long as she could, but watching her father's demise finally became too much to handle. She managed to say a prayer, kiss his forehead, and bid him goodbye. At seven o'clock, she returned home. She became our communications director, contacting those who needed to be updated on events as they developed. The calls she made between the nursing home and relatives were invaluable.

At 10:30, I phoned home to say Dad had died. She immediately called the brother who lived out of state. She tells how they both needed to talk, to cry, and to pray.

"We remembered the good times growing up in our house. We laughed at Dad's quirky habits. We agreed on how much we'd miss him."

While still on the phone with her brother, she recalls looking out the kitchen window that overlooked the deck. Here's how she described the next minute:

"I couldn't believe the sight before me. I blinked to clear my vision several times, took a deep breath and let out a soft whimper of surprise. There on the deck stood my father, looking back into the house. Right at me! He smiled, nodded, and vanished as quickly as he had appeared."

She tells how she began to cry before revealing what had just transpired. She also remembers asking, "Am I crazy? Is that possible? Was Dad really here?"

My oldest son states that he didn't know how to explain her vision but answered from his heart. "Dad loved all of us and our house. You know how strong a presence he held in all our lives. I believe his spirit came home one more time to say his goodbye. I believe he knew this was a difficult time for you. I believe it was his way of telling you everything was going to be all right."

To this day, my daughter claims, "It was magical. I'll never forget the love I felt that instant."

Three years later, whenever she's feeling down she thinks back to that night and that mysterious moment and is flooded with the same comfort and love.

—Helen Colella,
Evans, Colo.

2

Messages from the Dead

Communication with others is one of the essential characteristics of being human, of being alive. A person who still speaks to us, by whatever means, cannot be truly dead and gone, even if they are no longer present in our physical, earthly realm.

Messages between the worlds of the living and the dead take a variety of forms. They may be delivered directly by the voice of an unseen presence, or indirectly through a series of meaningful coincidences. Communication may be as dramatic as a telekinetic display witnessed by a roomful of people, or subtle as a previously unnoticed photograph. However they arrive, messages from the dead share an indefinable quality of wonder and significance for their recipients.

Mother's Last Gift

My mother, Sally Lee Young, passed away in March, 1979, at the age of 83. We had always been close and I helped her as much as possible in her later years.

Shortly after she died, I was with my daughter, Kay, at her house. Kay showed me a blanket that she bought on sale for $30. I liked the blanket very much, and felt it was a real bargain at that price. I wanted to get one too, but this was during a time when my husband and I were dealing with a lot of expenses, and I felt I could not spend the money.

My husband and I discussed it after we got home. I was in the hallway while he was in the adjacent living room. He told me to go ahead and buy the blanket, but I was still reluctant to do so.

As soon as he finished talking, I heard a voice in my right ear, as clear as any voice I've ever heard. It was my mother. "Hon," she told me, "go look in the red souvenir purse Earl brought me from Florida, and you'll find 20 dollars. Go and buy that blanket. You deserve it."

I turned around, almost expecting to see her. Of course, she wasn't there.

Mother lived with us off and on before she died, and many of her belongings were still at our house. After she died, I went through all of her purses to make certain that nothing of importance was left in them. I found nothing more than old photos and cards and such. Nevertheless, I went and looked in the tattered, worn purse she had indicated. To my amazement, there was a fresh, crisp $20 bill.

I added my own $10 to the $20 and bought the blanket. I thought of it as mother's last gift. I have not heard from her since.

—*Opal Dodd,*
Parsons, Tenn.

Bill Said Goodbye

My husband and I were living in Manhattan at the time of this event. It was many years ago, but the experience is one I will never forget. New York was in the midst of a severe storm, near blizzard conditions, and it was bitter cold. My husband was working late that night and I was trying to stay warm. I had just picked up a book to read, and noticed the time was 7:00 p.m.

I had no sooner settled into my chair to read when suddenly there was a series of loud crashing sounds—horrible banging noises coming from everywhere, the walls, ceiling, and the floor. I became frozen with fear.

Then the doorbell rang. I was so terrified I felt like I couldn't move. I finally got up the courage to answer the door.

"Western Union telegram for you," said the young man at the door. I managed to open it and was shocked to read that a friend had just passed away. I remarked to the young man that a very dear friend of mine had just passed away, and his name was Bill Andrews. The young man then asked me if I knew a Stella Andrews who lived on Long Island.

I said, "Yes, that is Bill's sister."

He could tell that I was upset by the news, and he said he had a telegram for her as well. Much to my surprise, he offered to drive me to her house to deliver her telegram.

When we arrived, she came to the door and invited us in. She seemed to be upset even before reading the telegram. I asked her if she was all right. She told me that, at approximately seven o'clock, she starting hearing a series of loud crashes and banging noises. She thought her house was going to fall apart. As we spoke at length, we discovered that we were both getting the noises at approximately the same time!

Was Bill Andrews trying to get our attention? If so, he certainly had it!

—Adria Gillis,
Long Beach, Calif.

Flying Ornaments

My mom died very suddenly in April 1993. It was very devastating to us all. She was never sick; her heart just stopped at 64 years.

On Christmas of that year, we gathered as a family and tried to enjoy the holiday the best we could. We had eaten, opened gifts, and were all relaxing in the living room.

As we were chitchatting, my father told us he had just read a book entitled *Sex After Sixty*. Just after he said that, two Christmas ornaments came flying off the tree—not dropping, due to heaviness or dry branches, but flying, landing halfway between the tree and the couch, approximately three or four feet. One of them was an ornament my niece had made at a young age. The other "flyer" was one my mom had made herself.

Everyone stopped talking, and just looked at each other, trying to believe and understand what just happened.

My father asked, "What was that?"

Nobody knew, but we all saw it. We decided it was my mom telling my dad she didn't like his statement. She was also telling all of us she will always be with us on Christmas and every day, even if only in spirit and in our hearts.

We've told people our experience. They look at us as if we're crazy. We feel that Christmas mystery was only meant for us to see, share, and believe. From that day on I truly started to believe in ghosts, spirits, and things of the unknown.

—*Lynn Klepp,*
Depew, N.Y.

Please Don't Fret

David Cathum and I spent the first seven years of our lives together. Our mothers were best friends and had lived next door to one another since they were babies. Neither David nor I had any siblings, so we thought of each other as brother and sister.

I missed David terribly when my family moved to London, England, but as children do, I quickly adjusted to my surroundings and made new friends. Mom corresponded with David's mother Mary, but he and I never wrote letters.

Dad got transferred back to Pennsylvania when I was 17. I hadn't seen David for ten years, and my memory of what he looked like was vague at best. I recalled him being a skinny kid with blond hair and blue eyes. I also remembered he used to call me by my pet name, Bunsy.

Dad, Mom, and I stayed at my grandmother's house while our own home was being built. One day, a few days after we arrived, I was alone in the kitchen. My parents had gone out and my grandmother was in her room taking a nap.

There was a tap on the back door. As soon as I opened it, I knew that the tall skinny guy with the light blond hair was David.

"Hi, Bunsy," he greeted me cheerfully as he thrust a small bouquet of yellow daisies into my hands. David and I both realized at that moment that everything was the same between us; we were still brother and sister.

That year, I was a senior in high school. David had graduated a year earlier and had gotten a job at a veterinarian's office. We had different interests. David had his work and a girlfriend, and I was busy with friends, my upcoming graduation, and choosing a college. Every so often, David would drop over and we would talk. David loved animals and hoped to breed dogs one day. He also talked about marrying and having a family. He loved his mom and grandmother deeply, but longed to know his dad, who had left them soon after David was born.

It was just past Valentine's Day when I last saw David alive. He brought me a rose and a box of candy, along with some exciting news. He had found his dad and was leaving the next day to drive across the country to Las Vegas to meet him. His mother had saved up enough money to buy David a car.

David left, and a month passed. One night I stayed up studying for an algebra test I was having the next morning and fell asleep at my desk. Suddenly, I woke up with a jerk and was astonished to see David standing in my room grinning at me.

"What are you doing here at three in the morning?" I asked sleepily.

"Bunsy," he said, "I'm happy now. Tell Mom, please don't fret."

"What?" I blinked, but he was gone. "I must be dreaming," I mumbled to myself as I turned off the light and flopped into bed.

Mom, Dad, and Grandma were already at the breakfast table when I dragged my tired bones into the kitchen. The 7:30 news had just come on the small black-and-white television sitting on the counter. As I poured myself a glass of orange juice, I heard the newsman say, "And now to local news: David Cathum, a local teenager, has been found shot to death in the Mojave Desert. The son of a California police chief has been arrested and charged with his murder."

I was stunned. David had been dead for over a week, yet I had seen him at three that morning. He had been real—solid, and dressed in jeans and a white T-shirt with a lion on it.

I told Mom and Dad about the message he had given me for his mom. Dad drove me over to her house before school. Mary started crying as soon as she saw me, but quieted down as she listened to my story.

When I gave her David's message, her face lit up with a peaceful smile as she whispered, "Thank you." She then went on to explain that when David had been small and had gotten upset or frightened, she would take him in her arms and say, "Please don't fret."

Mary also confirmed that when the police found him, he was wearing blue jeans and a white T-shirt with a gray mountain lion on the back.

—*Sunday Uher,*
Lantana, Fla.

In the Jacket

My husband died suddenly on March 1, 1974. That was payday, but his employer could not release his paycheck, nor could I write any check from the bank, until certain legal procedures for death at the state level had been done.

Since I don't keep cash at home, I was perplexed as to what I could do in the meantime. I recalled that my husband kept a small amount of cash somewhere in the basement for his personal use. It was hidden and we always joked about it. I looked and could not find it.

Then one day I was sitting at the kitchen table wondering what to do next. Suddenly I heard this voice saying, "Look in the pocket of my old hunting jacket, and give half of it to Debbie." (Debbie is our daughter.)

I immediately went to the basement and looked in the jacket. There was the cash—not a lot, but enough to tide me over temporarily.

I think our loved ones who may have some unfinished business look after us in death.

—*Name withheld,*
Alton, Ill.

True Pitch

I come from a family of singers. When my father was young, he played in a local country band and discovered that he had a knack for playing a multitude of instruments. As I grew up and for many years afterward, Mother and Daddy would host "musicals" in our home. Daddy would play the fiddle, guitar, piano, or organ, but a special treat was when he played his saw, using his fiddle bow to produce the lonely wailing tunes. Friends and neighbors would get together purely for the love of singing and playing. They played everything from gospel to bluegrass to pop, but the singing was usually some form of gospel songs.

Our family especially loved to sing together anywhere we were—home, car, campfire, hotel room. Daddy was a great a cappella singer who never admitted to having the ephemeral "perfect pitch," but he was close. He usually got his pitch from an "A" tuning fork.

The first family get-together after my father died was naturally a very sad time for the family. We had no spirit for singing because he had been the organizer and motivator for our songfests. Finally we agreed that we had to sing a few songs, if only to honor Daddy's memory.

My brother John said, "Give us an 'A,' Larry." Before Larry could produce his tuning fork and strike it, we all froze at the ringing sound that was heard by every person in the room. As the clear, single sound subsided, Larry struck his tuning fork and the pitch matched perfectly. We had no idea where it came from and it has never happened again.

Was Daddy's spirit still there with us? We believe so.

—*Lanita Bradley Boyd,*
Fort Thomas, Ky.

Vision of Roses

In 1978, my mother was very ill, and dying of cancer. I had to leave my own family to care for her and my sister, Viriginia Ann Krug, who was helpless and unable to care for herself as she had muscular dystrophy.

My mother mercifully passed away after her 84th birthday. My sister, who was very nearsighted, was lying in bed just a few days after our mother had passed, when all of a sudden, the most beautiful roses she had ever seen appeared on the ceiling above her.

My mother loved roses, so my sister said, "Mother, I know that's you, and as you are showing me these beautiful roses, I know you are all right."

After she said that, the roses slowly disappeared. We were both convinced it was our mother, letting us know she was happy. I still believe that, and it's a good feeling.

—*Dolores Behn,*
New Richmond, Ohio

Money from Heaven

My brother Peter never forgot my birthday, although we were usually separated by hundreds or thousands of miles. A card would always arrive with a crisp new bill—usually a 20. Peter's sudden passing, at age 36, devastated me. Two months later, on the eve of my 40th birthday, I thought sadly of how there would be no special greeting awaiting me the next day. Then I had a very vivid dream; in it, my brother assured me that he remembered the occasion and would send a gift.

The next day found me on vacation in San Francisco. After a day of exhaustive sightseeing, including many an uphill climb, my companion and I were looking forward to a rest back at the hotel. Inexplicably, instead of taking the shortest, most logical route, I insisted that we take a much longer way. While waiting for a traffic light to change, a gentle breeze blew something against my ankle. Looking down, I saw a crisp, new, 20-dollar bill.

Nine years later, I found myself rushing across the country to be at my father's bedside in the intensive care unit; Dad had suffered a heart attack and the prognosis was grim—our family was already thinking of the final arrangements. Three weeks had passed and he was still hovering between this world and the next. One day, instead of my usual lunch in the hospital cafeteria, I felt a compelling urge to get takeout for a nearby park that had been Peter's favorite. Relaxing there, I felt his presence. In my mind, I could hear him saying that the doctors were wrong, that Dad would recover, and he would show me a sign. Walking back to the hospital, something on the sidewalk caught my eye. I bent down and picked up two rolled-up bills. Outside was a single, and inside of it was a 50. "What an unusual combination," I thought.

Arriving back at the ICU, I was grateful, but hardly surprised, to learn that the crisis was over and Dad would fully recover. It was not until that evening that I realized the significance of the amount of the bills— 1951 was the year Peter was born.

—Marion Brenish,
San Diego, Calif.

A Curious Photo

After my brother Dennis was killed in a 60-foot fall from some scaffolding at a construction site during 1970, his pet St. Bernard began howling at night from his abode on the large front porch of my brother's home. On the morning of the fourth day following my brother's death, my sister-in-law discovered that the dog had hung himself by jumping over the porch railing. The ten-foot leash wasn't quite long enough for the dog to land on the driveway next to the porch. I wonder if my brother, in the confusion that often follows death, might have beckoned to his dog and caused it to jump over the railing.

Several weeks later, my sister-in-law noticed their box camera sitting on the dresser in a spare bedroom. Only one photo had been taken. Curious, she had the film developed and discovered that it was a photo of my brother (her husband) sprawled out on the floor with his dog lying next to him. My sister-in-law said she did not take the picture and is reasonably certain that no visitor to their home took the picture. The camera did not have a timing device for self-photos.

It is certainly a curious picture. I wonder if my brother was in some way sending a message that the dog was with him.

—Mike Tymn,
Depoe Bay, Oreg.

My First Encounter with a Ghost

I lost my mother in a car crash in the spring of 1966, when I was only 17. It was a single-car crash on a winding road, and only she and I were in the car. If my learner's permit had not just expired, I would have been the one killed. Though I knew I had not caused the crash, I lived with a guilt that never went away.

Dad carried his flame for Mama all the time I was away at college. I returned home to live with him and teach school part-time, because I could not afford a place of my own yet. This was in August 1971, and I was 23 years old.

I came home one afternoon and went to my bedroom to take a short nap. Dad was still at work. I did not fall completely asleep but was in that state of semiconsciousness when I heard the screen door on the back porch slowly open and slam shut. It was the sound of the old screen door we used to have when I was a child, not the storm door Dad had replaced it with a few years back.

I started to get up, but found that I could not move; it was as though a cotton-thick forcefield was holding me down, paralyzing my limbs. I couldn't open my eyes, although I was now totally awake. I heard bare feet walking heavily across the hardwood floor of the kitchen. It sounded exactly like Mama's heavy walk in the summer when she used to go barefoot around the house.

The footsteps came on through the living room and down the hallway, punctuated by the occasional scatter rug on the floor. I tried to scream, but I had no command of my voice. I could only lay there, waiting. I did not believe in ghosts and had no idea what was fixing to grab me.

My eyes were sealed shut, as if I were in a deep hypnotic trance. The specter entered my bedroom and stood there, watching me. Then she moved to my bedside. I was gripped with fear as she seized me up in her arms, hugging me. In her urgency, she obviously did not know just how strong a spirit she was. Mama had been a rawboned woman and I remembered her strong hugs.

Although I couldn't see her, I knew, without a shadow of a doubt, that this was the ghost of my dead mother. Then she said, in that voice I remember so well, "It's okay."

She slowly released me and turned away. I heard her walk back the way she had come—her unforgettable footsteps on the hardwood—and the screen door from my distant childhood flapped forever behind her.

I felt my body descend to my bed. I was back to normal and could open my eyes.

The hypnotic paralysis was gone. I lay there looking at the pattern in the lace curtains that filtered the chiaroscuro of the afternoon, slowly absorbing my first experience with the paranormal.

Since that fateful afternoon I have not felt any of the old guilt, and I am now a firm believer in ghosts.

—*Barbara Kay Daniel,*
Buffalo Junction, Va.

Johnny Morris Told Us

My partner Angela and I have both been "sensitive" for as long as we can remember. I tend to see or sense things, and she hears things. She often gets an inner voice speaking to her, giving her advice on whether or not to go ahead with a particular project. She always, but always, ignores this advice, and always, to her own considerable annoyance, the voice proves right.

Back in the 1990s we became close friends with the great television presenter Johnny Morris, of BBC's *Animal Magic* fame. The relationship started off on a business footing but very quickly developed into one of those special friendships that come along but once in a lifetime. We just seemed to click with Johnny right from first meeting him, and his incredible sense of humor, hospitality, and need for companionship meant that we were very soon either seeing him or talking on the telephone almost every day.

For five years everything was fine, surreal but exhilarating. Although Johnny was in his late 70s when we first met him, he was incredibly active and mentally alert for his age, and we became heavily involved in the hectic diary of appearances, orchestral concerts, broadcasts, and so on that was Johnny's raison d'etre.

Occasionally our conversations would touch on the supernatural, as he knew that we both had an interest and personal experiences in that field. Although he was an atheist like ourselves, he very much kept an open mind on the subject and was always interested to hear of any new phenomena that we experienced. He was particularly interested to know if I could see Eileen, his wife, who had died some ten years before. I always denied that I had seen her for fear of upsetting him, but in the latter years when there was some turmoil in his life, I often saw her standing in the doorway to the kitchen where we always settled for a chat at his home. Her appearance was in no way worrying; it was as if she was keeping a protective eye on him and happy that he had friends to help him through.

Johnny had his own taste of the paranormal in the form of an out-of-body experience late in life when he fell down a flight of stairs. He related to us how he felt himself starting to fall, then suddenly became aware that he was detached from his body, watching himself tumble down the stairs. The experience was only momentary but appears to have been sufficiently strong that his body was totally relaxed during the fall. Even at the age of 81, he was uninjured, though the severity of his descent down the staircase could well have killed him.

Toward the end of his life, Johnny became very ill and started slipping in and out of lucidity. Much to the concern of his family and friends, when he was admitted to a hospital he was effectively cut off from contact with us by a person claiming to be next of kin. Try as we might, none of us could obtain any information on his health or whereabouts, and this sad state of affairs lasted for some seven weeks.

Sometime earlier we had bought Johnny's car when he changed it for a new model. One day Angela was out driving in this car when a voice came through to her which she instantly recognised as Johnny's.

"I've done it, dear; I'm here."

Instinctively she answered out loud, "Is that you Johnny?"

"Yes, dear," came the instant reply.

A shiver went down her spine as she realized what she was hearing. If Johnny was talking to her now, he must be dead.

"Are you alright, Johnny?" she cautiously asked into the thin air.

"Oh yes, dear!" the voice replied. In its tone she knew instantly that Johnny had passed on, and that wherever he was, it was much better than the life he had left. All of his aches and cares had gone for good.

A short time after Angela got home she received a telephone call from Johnny's housekeeper to advise her that Johnny had died earlier that day.

Although Johnny died alone, it was a comfort that he was able to get through to let us know he'd passed. By the sound of his voice, he'd gone to an infinitely better place!

—*John Keene, with Angela Morris,*
Eldersfield, United Kingdom

Night Visitor

One night a few years ago, I dozed off while watching the television news. I was awakened suddenly and I saw a figure sitting on the couch across the room. Now I was wide awake.

How in the world did anyone get into my house? Here was a mature woman, gray hair pulled back, wearing a blue blouse and a gray skirt. I never met such a person.

I had no idea who she was. Or so I thought for a while.

The image lasted a minute or so, no attempt at a voice message or telepathy. Her eyes looked straight over my right shoulder. She looked rather sad; I might say downright unhappy.

The story did not impress my friends. They knew about my out-of-body experiences, and teased me with comments like, "Yeah, right—a lady visits you and you never saw her before!"

I tried to remember if I had ever known her. I didn't have much luck.

About two weeks later she was back. It was the same time of night, and she was dressed the same. While she was there I stared at her face and noticed one detail. She had a dimple on her chin that looked like the letter "C".

After she disappeared I ran into another room where I had a picture of this same woman I had taken at Fort Lewis, Washington. We were both in the army. There it was, plain as day: the dimple was the same as it was in January 1944!

We met in the craft shop. She was painting a picture, and I went to use the photo darkroom. I sat down next to her and I didn't have to say a thing. When our eyes met we both knew we were hopelessly in love. No questions, no doubts.

We walked in the training areas together, even got a pass to Olympia for dinner. She had only been in the army a month or two before she arrived at the camp as part of a unit that made bread daily for about 50,000 people. My stay at this post was rather short. We talked of our future plans, and we made some promises to each other. We would marry and go to art school in California.

When I told her I was being transferred to Fort Riley, Kansas, she was devastated. She actually became quite ill.

We promised to write. Our V-mails kept us together, hers from San Francisco and mine from France and Germany. I was reassigned and sent back to the states. Two of her letters followed me home to Detroit. I had sent her letters while she was in California. Then for some reason her letters stopped coming. After almost a year it was apparent that she had lost interest in me.

After I got home from service I told my dad about the sweet lady with the soft voice and blue eyes. He told me: "Go for it! Don't let her get away!"

Since I was living away from home and attending a local university, my mother hid Ginny's letters. After my dad passed away in 1952, some of his personal items were disposed of. My heartless mother threw away his World War I uniform, his razor, and other items that I would have cherished. With my father's personal effects were three letters from Ginny I never saw. If I'd known about them, we never would have separated.

I'm convinced we will meet again in some future lifetime. I have her picture looking down on me as I type.

I tried to locate Ginny many times. I sent letters through the Service Locator File in St. Louis, Missouri. They forwarded my letters to her, but never told me where she lived.

In 1989, I sent her a Christmas card with a self-addressed postcard enclosed. The card came back with the signature "Cheryl" and a short message that Ginny was deceased. A short time later Ginny chose her way of letting me know that she understood that I never forgot her.

—Dominic P. Sondy,
Muskegon, Mich.

Treasures and Trash

My mother-in-law Gertrude Buchbinder, may she rest in peace, was a tough little New York Jewish lady who traveled the world with her husband, "The Doctor," collecting trinkets along the way. Several years after she passed away at the age of 84, I decided it was time for me to clean out her battered Chinese jewelry box.

Going through the baubles and beads, I couldn't help but marvel at the eclecticism of her tastes, ranging from the treasure of a delicate filigreed gold hamsa (hand) to the trash of necklaces made from two-inch, white plastic globules strung together on fishing line.

A tattered sandwich bag containing orange beads came to hand, and I extracted a broken necklace with care. The beads appeared to be plastic and were dirty and peeling in places.

"Trash," I said out loud.

"Be careful with that, Sharon! It's very valuable!" my long-dead mother-in-law rasped in my ear.

Looking around, I could see only my reflection in the mirror. The house was quiet, and for once, even the dogs weren't barking. Yet I had heard her. Her

Messages from the Dead 53

voice was so close, it was as if she had been standing at my right elbow.

I placed the beads in a new sandwich bag and told my husband about the incident.

"I'm taking them to be examined," I told him. "Your mother was very clear that these were not trash."

When I entered the store, I received a warm greeting and response—until I pulled the sandwich bag out of my purse and told the jeweler I wanted them appraised. She raised a perfect eyebrow, picked up one of the flaking beads, and tapped it on the glass counter.

"They're plastic," she said.

"My mother-in-law told me they were valuable."

She shook her head. "In your dreams. But, tell you what, I'll take them in the back and look at one of the beads under a microscope."

A few minutes later, she returned with a bright red bauble in her hand, shaking her head.

"The beads are really dirty. They seem to be covered in layers and layers of hairspray. That's the stuff that's flakes off when you touch them. I've never seen anything like it, and if I hadn't seen it with my own eyes, I wouldn't believe it. These beads are red coral and must be worth at least $3,000."

That night, I dreamed of Gertrude and thanked her. She was laughing.

There were other hidden treasures in the old battered Chinese jewelry box, like an ivory choker and a length of light pink angel's wing coral. But the one

I wear the most is the red coral necklace, especially when I expect a tough day at work. As soon as I put them on, I know my feisty mother-in-law is beside me to help me get through the day.

—*Sharon Bell Buchbinder,*
Pikesville, Md.

The Key Is, "I Am"

My mother, Lollie Holland, died on the morning of New Year's Eve, 1999. Almost 90 years old, she was in poor health and ready to go. But it was hard for me to get used to not having her in this world, and I felt lost without her, knowing I would never see her again. I just could not seem to get on with my life. I felt I hadn't said a proper goodbye, or thanked her enough for giving me my life and teaching me how to appreciate it.

One day, several weeks after her funeral, I found myself very sleepy in the middle of the afternoon, and I lay down for a nap. I fell asleep almost immediately. Then I had a strange and very vivid dream. It seemed that the phone at my bedside rang and woke me up. I had been very deep in sleep, and I fumbled the receiver as I tried to answer, croaked "Hello" in a voice full of sleep, then managed to clear my throat and say "Hello" more clearly.

The response I got was astounding. It was my mother's voice, sounding young and strong again, and she said "Hello!" with amusement in her tone, as if she were enjoying my clumsy attempts to answer the phone. *It's Mother!* I thought, but I did not say anything aloud. What could I say: "How are you?" I knew how she was—she was dead!

After a short pause, she said, carefully, as if being sure to make herself understood, "This is the last good-bye in this life." Then she said something that has left me wondering to this day about what exactly she meant. Slowly and emphatically she said, "The key is, 'I am.'"

I thought immediately that this was a very important message, and I also had the impression that she was not supposed to be telling me this.

"I am?" I asked.

"The key is, 'I am,'" she repeated in the same deliberate, emphatic way. Then it seemed to me that someone else was near her, perhaps hearing her end of the conversation, because she broke off and made a joking remark in a light tone, and then she was gone.

The line wasn't just dead, it was absolutely silent, and I was instantly wide awake. I did not have the phone in my hand, so apparently the phone call had been a dream. But it was absolutely the most real dream of my life, and I knew beyond a doubt that the message from my mother was very important and very real. But what did it mean? I had the impression that it was something Mother had learned after her death, something she thought it would be helpful, maybe vital, for me to know.

When I told my partner, Beth O'Neal, about the dream, she said, "I think you can 'take it to the bank,' because I, I guess, prayed to Lollie and told her, 'Tony needs to know you're all right.'"

Maybe that dream was the answer to Beth's prayer, but if it was, it was more than just a reassuring message of farewell. It was also a clue to some greater meaning which my mother thought was so important that she contacted me from the other side of death to tell me.

Since then I've run across several references to "I am" in my reading. Once or twice, for a fleeting moment, I have grasped a meaning I can't really express. All I know is, my mother (for I do believe that she really did contact me from beyond the grave) gave me a message to help me in this life. It was a message like nothing I ever heard my mother say before, and I do believe she really wanted me to have "the key." I will keep trying to understand it, and some day that key may unlock a mystery.

—*Antoinette Azolakov,*
Austin, Tex.

3

Dream Visitations

It is not at all unusual to dream of people close to us who have died. I frequently have dreams about my grandparents who have passed away. For the most part, these have the qualities of "normal" dreams: abrupt, illogical changes of scene, people acting out of character, a jumble of old memories, recent events, and pure fantasy. As much as I would like to see and talk to my grandparents again, I don't feel they are really present in these dreams.

There is a class of dreams that is recognized as much different by those who experience them. "Visitation dreams," as they have been called, are much more focused and meaningful. The dreamer wakes feeling he or she has been in the presence of someone from the world beyond death. The dreamer usually experiences great comfort and reassurance, and may even bring back important messages for others, or information about the deceased that can be independently verified.

Dreams are a mysterious aspect of the human condition, and visitation dreams perhaps most mysterious of all.

My Father's Ring

My father, Charles Novit, died suddenly on August 29, 1997, at his home in Cutchogue, New York. His death came only weeks after the deaths of my husband and my stepmother.

Because I lived such a distance away, I could only attend my father's wake for one day. When I arrived at the funeral home, I noticed right away that my father was wearing a gold wedding band on his left ring finger. The ring seemed to be too large for him, but because his hands were badly gnarled from arthritis, and because he had lost weight over time, I didn't think much of it.

About a month after my father's death, I awoke after having a strange dream in the middle of the night. In the dream, I saw my father exactly as he had looked in the funeral home, complete with the too-large ring on his finger.

"Diane, be careful. You're going to lose your ring," my father told me in the dream. Then I woke up.

All that day the dream, and my father's words, stayed with me and puzzled me. Why would I dream that my father's ring was mine—and why would he warn me about losing something that was not mine to lose?

Later that day, my stepsister, Kathryn Hartman, phoned me. During the course of our conversation, she asked me, "Diane, do you remember the ring Pop had on when he was laid out?" Of course I remembered, and I was all ears!

"I've meant to tell you this before, but I kept forgetting," she said. "I found out why that ring didn't fit him."

Some time before he passed away, Kathy told me, my father had informed my niece that the ring actually belonged to his father—my grandfather. After I left the funeral home that day, the girl told Kathy. And Kathy, thinking that my father would have wanted me to have the ring, slipped it off his finger.

"Because it's small I forgot where I put it the first time. Then I found it again, and lost it again, several times. But I just found it again yesterday, and put it away in a safe place so I know where it is. I'll give it to you the next time we get together."

Then I told her about the dream I had, just the night before. The best we could figure was that my father did indeed want me to have the ring, and wanted both of us to know it. He certainly made his point. That dream is something I will never forget, and the ring is now safely tucked away in my possession.

—Diane Crawford,
Lake Ronkonkoma, N.Y.

Kind Voices from the Past

Fifteen years ago, I was battling a depression so awful, I wanted to kill myself. My husband had used me as a punching bag too many times, so I packed up my children and moved to another state, where I hoped we could make new and more peaceful lives for ourselves.

But it didn't work. Jake followed us. Around Christmastime, he took the children from me, and I had no idea where they were. None of my so-called friends would help me find them. Within three days, I lost the house where we had been living, my car, and most important of all, I lost my children. I felt as though there was no one I could trust.

I was angry and depressed, and I could find no one who would help me. I didn't want anyone who knew me to see me reduced to living on the streets, so in the middle of a frozen January, I began to hitchhike across the country. It was a death wish that prompted me to do this. Somewhere along the way, I hoped I would die, either from exposure to the cold, or exposure to some thug, who would take it on himself to do to me what I didn't have the courage to do to myself.

It didn't work. I made it all the way to California, and I was still alive! There, in my wanderings, I met a fellow who was camping out on a mining claim—a beautiful wooded piece of land, away from the rest of society. I stayed there for a time, as it was easier to commune with the trees than it was to talk with people. In fact, I had been hurt so badly, I wanted nothing to do with people. But the man I was with was lonely and hurting too, and well, it's an old story—I became pregnant.

At first, I wanted to get an abortion, because I didn't believe I could take care of a child—I couldn't even take care of myself. But something happened that made me feel that keeping the child I was carrying would be a good thing. I had a visitation—actually, two of them. The first one came when I was alone and had fallen asleep in the shelter we shared. Whether I was half asleep, or dreaming, I don't know. A kind man came to me, and talked of his experiences during the Civil War. He told me of a passenger boat that had been sunk, and how horrible it was. "But that's what war is," he said. He talked on, and on. The last thing he said was, "A lady shouldn't sleep with her boots on. Let me help you take them off."

I awoke with a start, and he was gone. When I described this to the man I was with, he said, "That was my great-great-grandfather. He worked for President

Lincoln, and he would have known all those things." I don't know why he came to me that way. Whether he was telling me that the baby I was carrying came of good people, or whether the son I gave birth to was the reincarnation of this man, I never will know for certain.

But it was the second visitation that helped me to heal. My grandfather, who had been dead many years, came and shared stories of his childhood with me. I told him how terrible I felt over my situation. "I understand," he told me.

These were the best words he could have said. It took a long time to heal, spiritually and emotionally. But that was the beginning of the process.

—Mary Ann Rau,
Arundel, Me.

Grandpa's All Right

The story that I will share with you has to do with my grandfather on my mother's side of the family. He had Alzheimer's, and my granny died before he did, so my family was left with the only choice that they felt that they had—to place him in a nursing home. Well, to make a long story short, the nursing home abused him and that was what killed him in the end. They have since been shut down by demand of several patients' family members.

Anyway, about two or three months after his death, I had a dream where he was in our kitchen and I was walking toward him. I had "woken up," and walked through the hallway into the kitchen where the table is, and he was sitting in one of the swivel chairs at the kitchen table. He swiveled the chair and got up and came toward me with his arms outstretched and a warm, loving smile on his face. For some reason that I don't know, I became frightened and told him that he was dead and to go away and that he wasn't supposed to be here. At that point he stopped walking toward me and large tears began to slide down his cheeks and his arms were still outstretched, then he just disappeared like a wisp of smoke.

I then woke up for real and was amazed at how real that dream seemed. The very next night I had the same dream, except this one took up where the other one left off. I "woke up" and went into the hallway. There he was, standing with big tears rolling down his cheeks and his arms open as if he wanted a hug from me.

This time, however, I approached him and hugged him and told him that he belonged with Granny up in heaven. Then he smiled at me, and he conveyed to me to tell everyone he loved them, and especially to tell my mother that he didn't hold anything against her for putting him in the nursing home. He understood that it was the only option that she had at the time and that he knew that she had done the best she could do under the circumstances. He told me to tell her that he loved her, and that he was going to be with Granny in heaven and that everything was going to be all right. Then he disappeared again.

The next day, when I told my mom about the dream and what he had told me to tell her, she just burst into tears and hugged me fiercely. I was only 15 at the time, and I had no idea if I had just made her cry because she was upset at something I said or because she was happy!

She sat down and told me that she had not been sleeping well, and she had been making herself physically sick with the guilt that she felt because of her decision to put my granddad in the nursing home, and so in essence she felt responsible for his death. She told me that with what I had just told her (and she knew it was real because I wouldn't have known about how she was upset and all, because she had been trying to hide it and had been keeping it inside for months on end) I had probably added some years to her life by lifting that huge burden off her shoulders!

I knew then that I had a special gift and that God had given it to me so that I could comfort those who needed it the most.

—*Trish Cody,*
Fayetteville, Ark.

Heed Your Dreams

My husband Jim and I were intrigued by studies indicating that people dream as many as five dreams per night. Unless we write them down after waking, we usually forget them. So we kept pens and pads on our bed tables and recorded our dreams while they were fresh in our minds.

Interpreting them was confusing inasmuch as symbols don't always have the same meaning to everyone. To help us understand, we bought and studied numerous books on the subject. It was always exciting to experience déjà vu and trace events back to earlier dreams.

Since we believed dreams were a gift of the Holy Spirit, we felt is was God's way of helping us cope with life. Our belief stemmed from Biblical stories where prophets avoided adversity by heeding their visions and dreams—such as the story where Joseph interpreted Pharoah's dreams and saved the Egyptians from starvation during a seven-year drought.

While dreams are helpful, they don't reveal everything. My husband's premature death following surgery caught me completely unprepared. After adjusting to the shock, I sought a way to ease my grief. It seemed logical to me that Jim would contact me through dreams if such communication were possible. And he did.

Usually he said little, if anything, but he looked so healthy and vibrant that I felt consoled. I knew that he was home with God. While that was a comforting thought, it didn't allay my loneliness. I missed our marriage partnership and wondered why I had been left behind. For two years I kept busy with family, church, reading, and writing.

One night, I prayed for a sign telling me what I should do with the rest of my life. After I fell asleep, I had a lucid dream where Jim appeared and embraced me. My senses were so enhanced, I smelled his aftershave and felt the warmth of his lips.

"I love you, Sally, but it's time for me to go on to a higher plane." I heard his voice clearly. "Your grieving is hampering my transition. I'll always love you and care for you, but I must move on, just as you must start a new life for yourself."

As if viewing a movie, I watched angels appear on each side of Jim and escort him out my front door. Still dreaming, I heard hammering in my kitchen. I went there and found a tall, slender man, his face concealed by a huge letter "E," replacing my back door.

"Don't be afraid and don't worry. I'll keep you safe and take care of you for rest of your life," the man assured me in a voice I didn't recognize.

Still smelling Jim's aftershave, I awakened with the vision etched clearly in my mind. I lay quietly trying to interpret my dream. The part about Jim ascending to a higher place was understandable. But what about the stranger whose face was concealed behind the letter "E"?

I waited and waited for Jim's next dream appearance to gain an explanation. Days passed into weeks, but Jim no longer materialized in my dreams.

During that time a friend introduced me to her widowed cousin, an intelligent, attractive man with a delightful sense of humor and engaging personality.

After a year's courtship, we married. A few weeks later, Jim appeared in a dream. He didn't speak, but his captivating smile told me that he approved of my marriage to Mel Engeman.

—*Sally Kelly-Engeman,*
Loveland, Colo.

Lest I Forget Thee

When my parents divorced in the 1960s I drifted away from my father. I finally rekindled our relationship in 1990. His personal religious feelings had never been clearly expressed to me, even after we reunited, but remained a very private part of his life.

In March 1993 my father began losing a difficult and lingering battle with cancer. It became painfully clear that his time was short as he withered in the care of medical staff in a hospital he had sworn never to enter.

We talked briefly during hospital visits, when he was lucid and comfortable. Once or twice I tried to explain to him what I had experienced from my own recent near-death experience caused by a poisoning incident. I spoke of the love and the peace that had I found on the other side. He scoffed at my ideas and told me to quit talking about such things that were only in my imagination. "When you're dead you're dead!" he said adamantly.

As a World War II veteran he had seen more death than most people. He didn't expect anything beyond the grave. No reward. No punishment. Just release from the horror of cancer.

My brothers and sisters were called to the hospital late one night after the failure of a final, desperate surgery to stop my father's bleeding. His heart, weakened from numerous heart attacks, simply failed. He passed while unconscious.

Each member of the family was allowed to enter the room where his remains waited for a personal, final farewell. His wishes were for immediate cremation, so this would be my last visit with my father. As I kissed his forehead, I sensed his presence in the room. The body before me was just a worn, decimated vehicle that he had outgrown.

In that brief moment I prayed for his release from earthly bonds, and used a memorized section from the *Tibetan Book of the Dead* to direct him toward the light.

The room seemed so empty at the end of those prayers. I was convinced he was off to a new and pain-free adventure.

Over the next six years a few of my family members sensed my father's presence by catching a fading mist seen from the corner of the eye, by hearing a word whispered here and there, and often through his visits in dreams. In an Irish-American family these things are quite common, and spoken of within the family bounds.

In September 1999, I had my first clear assurance that he still stood beside me, and helped as he could.

My work as an emergency-management consultant, preparing communities for disasters and recovery, often required me to be deskbound or wasting away in continuous meetings. I needed some form of exercise, outside of the occasional gym work, to keep fit. My work drive after my father's passing had turned me into a workaholic, with only rare moments of personal relaxation. It became obvious that if I didn't find active physical hobbies I would suffer from lack of rest and from being overweight.

After doing an analysis of the types of sports I was still fit to perform, I chose kayaking. Not the bold, whitewater madman approach, but more of the open lake ventures that allowed some fishing and photography from the kayak, and some isolated camping forays. After visiting local kayak outfitters I was ready to start my new avocation. I then paid a substantial sum for lessons at a state-managed aquatic center in Folsom, California.

The night before my initial training class I had a distressing and vivid dream. Whenever these had occurred to me in the past I found them to be strong warnings of events to come—especially those that promised a threat to my health and safety. In this dream my father came to me and gave me a very stern warning not to take the kayak lessons.

I awoke shaken, fully drenched in sweat. The rest of the night was filled with restless anxiety and worry. I could not afford to just throw away the nonrefundable class fees. Yet, my father's words were so insistent.

My phone call with the instructor at the aquatic center was memorable. I couched my situation as carefully as I could. I explained the intense feelings I had that this was not a good idea to continue, and I requested to reschedule the training. That simply was not allowed. "That's the rules," he said. So, against all my financial conservatism, I cancelled the full-day training course and forfeited the fees.

Several months later, in January 2000, I told this story to my cardiologist as I was recovering from open-heart surgery. In September, when I was planning to take the kayak course, I had no inkling of the time bomb ready to go off in my chest. Until I collapsed just after Christmas, I had no indications of how close I was to a massive heart attack. I thought it was bronchitis I had contracted after a visit to relatives in Indiana during Thanksgiving.

My doctor made it very clear that if I had taken the kayak course I would most likely have had a catastrophic heart attack while submerged, since the course required turning the kayak upside down and then inverting the craft upright while inside of it. Whether it was my subconscious warning me, or my father, the doctor assured me that my reluctance to take that class saved my life.

There is no doubt in my mind that my father was watching over me and warning me from the other side.

—*Patrick Tobin,*
Spring Branch, Tex.

Only the Best

The only person in the family who seemed to really care about and love me was my beloved grandmother, Karoline Becker. I can't remember a harsh or mean word from her mouth—quite in contrast to other family members who enjoyed gossiping about everyone, including their own relatives. The worse the mishap, the better.

It felt like a silent but strong support with my grandmother just being there, reassuring me of her love without words.

What a nightmare when one day, not long before Christmas, her old body just couldn't do it any longer and she passed away.

"Why her? Why couldn't it just have been you?" my mother sobbed, but her words didn't hurt me. I had had heard worse, and besides, nothing could top the terrible emptiness that filled me completely.

I managed to get through my remaining teenage years without too many troubles with my mother, probably because I decided to move out before things could escalate. Desperately looking for love, I hoped to find a loving partner. But my love life was a disaster. Careerwise I couldn't complain. Everything was falling into place seemingly by itself, and I landed a great job that brought me overseas a lot.

Then, in Barbados (one of my favorite destinations), something strange happened. As so often happens, I spent my evening surrounded by colleagues, but still alone. I decided to call it a night early. Before falling asleep I sadly admitted to myself that it obviously wasn't meant to be for me. I clearly was to spend the rest of my life loveless. I was then in my mid-20s with a string of terribly failed relationships behind me.

When I was deep asleep I had a visit from my grandma. She looked beautiful and healthy. I would have guessed her to be in her 60s. (She was 81 when she passed on.) She was covered in a beautiful green light that spread over my bed and myself. It actually seemed to fill the whole room.

Grandma sat down at the edge of my bed beside me and I clearly recall having a conversation with her. Not in the usual way, however; her lips weren't moving, but I could clearly hear her even though there were no words or sounds. She was talking in pictures.

My bed, situated in a tiny room, was quickly moving toward the wall. There was an old wooden wardrobe that now opened its doors; grain came pouring out of it, quickly filling the floor and the space up to my bed, and spilling all over my feet. Grandma smiled and I felt so unspeakably good. I felt everything would be all right.

The next morning I just knew it wasn't an ordinary dream. I knew this visit was real, but its real message I had yet to learn.

A short time later, after swearing myself to never, ever get involved with the opposite sex again, I met someone very special under the most unbelievable circumstances. The moment we laid eyes on each other we knew we were destined for each other. Within weeks we had moved in together. Six months later we got married, and within two years we had two lovely daughters.

Thanks heaps, Grandma!

—A. T. Meissl,
Tewantin, Queensland, Australia

Visit from Susan

I awoke from my dream in tears, sobbing and hugging the rolled-up blanket. My late wife Susan had returned to visit just a little more than a year after passing over.

Our 20-year marriage had not been good. Actually, it had evolved into a living nightmare. Susan was an alcoholic, and this affliction led to a rough life both for us and for our son. It led to a hard and painful death for her.

In the weeks before she died, Susan tried to tell me how much she regretted the way things had turned out. Once she hugged me hard and cried.

"I'm so sad that you're going to feel more relief than sorrow when I'm finally gone," she said.

"No, it's not that way, Susan." I consoled.

"But it is," she replied. "If I were in your shoes that's exactly what I'd feel! Relieved! And I'm sorry. I'm so sorry!"

She was right. I couldn't ever fool her. The day she died I did feel a sense of relief. I was relieved that there would be no more of her hallucinating and incoherent ramblings. I was glad that she wouldn't be there to criticize, condemn, and complain. There would be no more of her night-long ranting to keep me from sleep. No more tantrums, no more fighting, no more suicide attempts. No more pain.

But at the same time, she was wrong. In those last years of insanity I had forgotten all about the adventurous young woman I had married. I had forgotten about the gal from Mississippi who had once been so enthusiastic about showing her new Yankee husband how to use a shrimping and crabbing net that she had rushed laughing into the tidal marshes of Savannah, Georgia, only to become trapped in muck up to her knees. I had focused only on the Ms. Hyde she eventually became. Only after all the drama and turmoil had subsided did I remember the real Susan. Somewhere along the line I had hardened my heart against her. I had let her slip away day by day, and I felt so sad and guilty. But on January 25, 1999, it was too late to change anything.

Thirteen months later, Susan appeared in an intense dream. I usually can't recall my dreams, but this was a rare exception. She managed to slip into a dream that was already in progress. As soon as I recognized her, everything else fell away. It was just her and me. I broke into tears because I missed her so much and I felt so badly about being angry with her most of the time that we had been together.

She put her arms around me to provide comfort, but I continued to sob uncontrollably. I tried to tell her how much I loved and missed her, but I couldn't choke the words out. It didn't matter. She knew the score.

"It's okay, Angel; they told me you would be like this but I wanted to drop in on you anyway. I just wanted to tell you everything is okay. You don't have to worry about a thing. You've been so good. Everyone over here is happy with the way you've been playing the game. Believe it or not they're pretty happy with me too! It's all going according to plan. We all play our roles."

I continued crying and held her as tightly as I could.

"You're playing a good game, Angel. Just keep on plugging. Everything is working out as planned. You're doing good. I gotta go now. I'll see ya later."

When she said that I wept even harder and tried to hold onto her, but she just faded away and was gone.

I woke up clasping the rolled-up comforter and crying real tears.

So what happened? Buried grief and guilt erupting from my subconscious? Had I been reading too much Sylvia Browne, or had this been a real visit from Susan? All I know is, I don't usually remember my dreams, and even when I do I don't wake up crying and hugging a blanket. It felt like she had really been there.

—*Thomas P. Sweeney,*
Rolling Meadows, Ill.

Thanks, Ralph

My mother Miriam and her friend Ralph Russo of 36 years would come to my home every Sunday for dinner and good conversation, and of course my mom would see her granddaughters. Ralph and I would watch a show called *Mystery of the Bible* when they would come. That started some good conversation between us. Sometimes it would get a little heated, too.

You see, I am Jewish and Ralph was Catholic. The main subject was always about who the Messiah is. Jews do not believe Jesus was the Messiah and Catholics do. It never got out of hand, but I guess we both had fun getting each other a little hot under the collar.

This went on for a few years. Then one day my mother told me Ralph had had a stroke. I myself was very sick at that time and never did I get to see him at his wake, nor could I go to the funeral due to my illness. I was so sad because I never got a chance to say goodbye the way I would have liked to.

A little more than a month passed. One night I had a dream. Ralph was in it, and the first thing I asked Ralph was, "Was Jesus Christ G-D?"

Ralph said, "G-D is the creator of all things."

I asked Ralph again, "Is Jesus Christ G-D?" and again Ralph said, "G-D is the creator of all things."

Dreams often change very quickly, as mine did. The next thing I saw, Ralph was at a distance from me and all I could make out was that Ralph had on a black shirt and white collar. I said to myself, "Is Ralph a priest here?"

As I started to walk closer to him I noticed he was not a priest. His shirt was one of those two-tone colored shirts that was black with a white collar and white cuffs.

My dream shifted quickly again and I found myself sitting on a stone wall. Sitting on the wall, Ralph walked up to me to say goodbye. I kissed him on the neck as I hugged him with tears in my eyes as he walked away. All of a sudden I woke up from my dream and had tears running down my cheeks.

I called my mother later that day to tell her that Ralph came to me in my dream and told her everything about it. When I got to the part about Ralph's black shirt with the white collar and cuffs, she asked me to repeat that and I did. My mother got very quiet and then sounded very sad as she said to me, "We went out to eat that night before his stroke and I told him how handsome he looked that night." The last shirt Ralph wore the night before his stroke was a black shirt with a white collar and white cuffs.

I knew then and there that my dream was real and that I got to say goodbye the way I wanted to.

Thanks, Ralph.

—*Philip L. Brodsky,*
Yonkers, N.Y.

Grandma Lilly

Growing up in an Irish Catholic household in Oregon in the 1960s, I was fortunate to have my paternal grandmother Lilly (Mary Lillian Kelleher) living with us. She was a force of nature in spite of her diminutive size, and her wrath was legendary in our home; she swore alternately in English and Gaelic. Her laughter was equally memorable and contagious. She was my favorite person in the entire cosmos growing up. Everyone who knew her had a book's worth of stories about her, and a collection of her pithy quotes. I can still vividly picture her knitting in her rocking chair while I sat on her footstool talking about the old days, the new days, and everything in between.

At Sunday mass she would pray her rosary, peripherally aware of the rest of the service. She was a believer in dreams, omens, and the spiritual realm. She dreamed of the Kennedy assassination before it happened, as well as other lesser occurrences. My father always joked with her, making her promise not to dream about him. He confided that she had "gifts" that were probably passed on from our ancestors.

After being clinically dead during a cancer operation, Grandma Lilly told me about meeting her own grandmother and her parents, and eagerly trying to reach them only to be told that it wasn't her time yet. She told me that she returned here very reluctantly, which troubled and baffled my young mind.

Inevitably I grew up and moved out, and eventually Grandma Lilly wore out and decided she had lived long enough. At 88, or 89, or 90—no one was quite sure exactly; she was a little coy about her true birthdate—she passed on.

Eight years later as my wife Kate and I prepared for the birth of our first child, we bickered endlessly on which boy's name to choose for our firstborn son, although we didn't know the sex for certain. Although it was mostly amiable and lighthearted, we are both very stubborn, and we dug in our heels on our respective choices.

Exactly six weeks before my wife's due date I had an amazing dream. I was back in my parents' house. I was grown up, but the interior looked exactly as it had when I was young. And there was my Grandma Lilly rocking away. She looked up and beckoned me to the footstool. I sat down and told her how thrilled I was to see her. She took my comments in stride, and we talked about mundane things as though we had never stopped. Then she said she had to leave and that I should, too. As I hauled myself up from the footstool, now much smaller than I remembered, Grandma Lilly looked up over her knitting and casually spoke a few words that even now raise the hairs on the back of my neck. "Oh, by the way—you do know that it's going to be a girl, don't you?"

"No!" I stammered. "Thank you for telling me!"

I woke up and looked at the clock. It was 4:00 a.m.; nevertheless, I woke my wife and told her exactly what had happened. She later told me that it wasn't being awakened and told this fantastic dream that got her; it was the absolute steadfast conviction in my voice at the wonderful visitation.

From that moment on, we dropped the argument over boys' names and vigorously debated girls' names. Six weeks later our daughter was born. My wife looked at me wide-eyed for a moment as she remembered the dream. Regaled with various stories about my grandmother, she made sure we thanked her for watching over the birth and sharing her wisdom with us.

I'm sorry to say there are already Lillies in the family, so we didn't name Christa for her. I think that there's some of Lilly in her all the same, and I am sure some of the "gifts" have been passed on. Christa shares my interest in and love of the supernatural and is a devoted reader of FATE magazine, as am I.

—Dan Kelleher,
Tigard, Oreg.

Or Was It Just a Dream?

As a preteen caretaker for my 90-year-old grandfather, who lived next door me, I heard many of his stories. Most were humorous. This one, told often, had a different tone. As an adult, while cleaning out a box of family letters and photos, I came across bits and pieces of the story again.

In 1918, 40-year-old Fred Hahn of Bluffton worked in the oil and gas fields of northwestern Ohio. He was a pumper for the Ohio Oil Company, which eventually become Marathon Oil. His was physical work and he enjoyed being outdoors. He and his wife, Bertha, were parents of five children, ages 4 to 18.

Fred's brother Harry, 33, was single and engaged to be married. He and his fiancée had selected material for Harry's wedding suit. They had purchased several pieces of kitchenware in preparation for setting up a home. Harry lived in Fostoria, about 30 miles north-west of Bluffton.

Fostoria was a railroad town in the golden era of railroading. Harry had worked for the Big Four (Cleve-land, Cincinnati, Chicago, and St. Louis) Railroad since 1910. During the summers he played semi-professional baseball in towns like Tiffin, Bucyrus, Findlay, and Fostoria.

Harry loved his work, but there were times dur-ing the winter when, as in his own words in a letter to Fred, it was tough: "a week ago Saturday [I] worked out in it all day and I'll say it was terrible and [on the] R.R. you get it worse than any thing else. Everybody froze their selves somewhere; we had a Big 4 freight engine and one passenger engine to get out. I walked in snow knee-deep the length of two engines and I had to feel for the Pullman as my eyes were frozen shut and I could not see. I froze my eyes and face."

For Fred and Harry, it was the best of times. As hard workers from no-nonsense German-Lutheran backgrounds, they shared many common values: love of family, the outdoors, animals, and physical labor. Fred and Harry were as close as any two brothers, as a collection of their letters from the span of 1910 to 1918 demonstrates.

No time existed for unexplained coincidences, psychic phenomena, or dream interpretation. Despite that, one dream during Fred's lifetime was unlike any other experienced in his eventual nine decades of living and dreaming. It came to him as a call from the darkness one night in early December 1918.

Fred dreamed that Harry tried to call him but couldn't make contact. The dream captivated Fred's imagination the rest of his life. Trying to find the sense in it, however, always failed.

In the very early morning hours of Wednesday, December 5, 1918, the night of Fred's dream, Harry was uncoupling freight cars. His only communication with the engineer was with his red-globed kerosene lantern. The engineer interpreted Harry's signal incorrectly. While Harry signaled to pull forward, the engineer slipped the big black locomotive in reverse. Before Harry could safely jump aside, the huge, 2-8-0 locomotive, with 57-inch driving wheels, backed the train into Harry, cutting off both his legs at the knees.

All of this was unknown to Fred even the next morning as he sat with his wife at the breakfast table and shared details of his dream. He couldn't make sense of it. The dream was out of the ordinary, and it bothered Fred.

Eventually Fred finished breakfast, hitched his horse Al to his work wagon, and headed to the oil field.

Later that day a telephone call came to the Hahn home. The caller was from Bucyrus. Harry was dead; killed shortly after midnight. The caller apologized. He had tried unsuccessfully all night long to get through. The lines never connected. Although only two counties separated Bluffton from Bucyrus, completing a long-distance telephone call in 1918 wasn't simple. It required manual patching by a series of operators, from one phone system to the next and so on.

For the rest of his life Fred told the dream and death story, which left each listener spellbound. In his later years, Fred embellished the story, making it less tragic. He even claimed that Harry sat up in the ambulance and smoked a cigar on the way to the hospital. But it didn't happen that way and he knew it. Harry died instantly, his body severed by the cold steel wheels of the freight car.

After the funeral, in a letter to Fred's wife from Harry's former fiancée, the young woman wrote: "I wish I could have had a talk with him before he died."

Certainly Fred shared the same wish. At the same time he must have wondered: "Was Harry trying to contact me, or was it just a dream?"

—*Fred Steiner,*
Bluffton, Ohio

4

Near-Death and Out-of-Body Experiences

If there is some part of us (the soul or spirit) that survives physical death, it would seem logical to conclude that consciousness is somehow able to exist independently of the body. In fact, the experience of countless individuals suggests that awareness can and does leave the body, even before death.

Out-of-body experiences (OOBEs) can happen spontaneously, without warning. It has also been asserted that leaving the body at will is an ability that can be learned. Out-of-body explorers may travel through the physical world, or they may visit other dimensions, the astral or etheric planes. The observation of astral travelers may be responsible for some ghost reports.

Near-death experiences (NDEs) are the subject of a growing body of literature, both scientific and anecdotal. The phenomena reported by persons who have died, or come close to death, and returned to the world of the living often parallel descriptions of the afterlife in religious literature, but usually do not fit the beliefs of a given tradition in all details.

NDEs almost always have a profound effect on those who have them. Most experiences report an expanded sense of purpose, increased compassion for others, and freedom from the fear of death. Similarly, those who undergo a spontaneous OOBE often experience a dramatic shift in their worldview and take a much greater interest in metaphysical topics.

A Mysterious Journey

I write this true account in hopes that it will touch the depths of you and open your eyes about the afterlife.

One day at the swimming pool, when I was nine years old, I believed I was old enough to test my limits. I meandered over to the deep end, only to find that the depth was too much for me. I was swallowed in as I slid further down under, unable to keep myself afloat.

My body was under water, but my spirit felt as if it was being lifted above the scene.

Everything became pitch black around me as a powerful wave of energy formed a hole in the void and swirled around in an array of many colors. At the very end of this tunnel, I could see white light and a radiant man coming toward me. His white robe flowed like the graceful wind; his hair was dark, wavy, and long, and his eyes pierced me with a magnificent blue.

He comforted me as we sat and talked for a while. I noticed that, although his mouth moved, he did not breathe or have any need to do so. The utmost feeling of peace and comfort encompassed me, and I pleaded with him not to have to go back to the cruel world. He said to me that I had a certain purpose to fulfill for the Spirit, which I had yet to discover.

Our conversation shifted as he told me to look around into the white space and view it in a different perspective. Suddenly, magical dome structures appeared all around us, reflecting various colors of the rainbow almost like crystal prisms. They were massive, with a very good flow of energy between them, and as I walked deeper into this wonderland they changed colors. I remember feeling a sudden calm and collectedness, and my eyes flung open as my physical body lay on the side of the pool, arms spread out wide.

I had taken a mysterious journey and come back to tell the story of my dying. My life has never been the same since that incident. Now I have the ability to look at things in a different perspective.

—Brian L. Sours,
Fort Wayne, Ind.

A Trip to Kansas City

I was in my twenties when I experienced my only astral projection. The night began comfortably for me in Tulsa. My husband Joe had already gone to sleep. I dozed also, and then realized I was flying.

I decided I'd like to see my friend Liz, who had just gotten married. She lived in Kansas City, Missouri, but it seemed very tangible to me. I took off in the air at high speed in the direction of Kansas City. The wind was riffling my hair and nightgown as I "flew." I zeroed in on an apartment building. Suddenly, I was in a room. I saw Liz asleep and an older man who was also asleep. I looked around her apartment before flying home.

I found myself on top of my mobile home. The rest of the night was languid, watching the night scene in the mobile park from my perch. Later, in a letter, I described what I'd seen of Liz's husband and her apartment. She was astonished, but verified my accuracy.

I remember the world got light and I looked down on my body. The next minute I was in my body. I was surprised I wasn't tired from my night-long trip. I haven't had an astral trip since that time.

I sometimes think I brought with me a memory from another realm.

—*Sharon Rice,*
Tulsa, Okla.

Dreams in the Attic

I grew up in Rochester, New York. When I was a child, my family thought our house was haunted. There were many reasons for this. We heard sounds in the middle of the night, had visions of what were thought to be ghosts, and felt certain sensations in different rooms of the house.

I had some encounters with these strange happenings as well, but there is one incident that I remember best. When I was about five years old, I had dreams of voices calling me to the attic. Sometimes there was more than one voice, but there was always one that stood out the most. It sounded like a man's voice. It was very deep, and instead of being scared of it, I felt a lot of comfort when I heard it.

One night I dreamed of the same voices calling me up to the attic as usual, but this time, I acted on what they wanted me to do. In my dream, I got out of bed and went to the attic door, which was in the corner of my bedroom. I opened the attic door. It was nighttime, but it wasn't dark enough to obscure my vision.

There was a window on the left side of the staircase that went into the attic. It was broken, and there was a clear plastic bag covering it. I climbed up the stairs of the attic. They were warped and all broken up. When I reached the attic, I noticed that it was small, and it smelled musty. We never used it, so whatever was up there had been up there for many years. The wood floor of the attic was rotten, and a lot of the floorboards were missing. Still hearing the voices calling me, I saw hands coming out of where the floorboards were absent. This must have startled me, because I woke up.

The next morning I told my mother of my experience. She told me that I shouldn't be scared, and she brought me to the attic to prove it. I was a little wary of going in again, but I did it anyway. As we walked up the stairs to the attic, I noticed that everything was the same as it was in my dream—even the broken window. The only thing missing was the ghosts. I was amazed.

After that I had dreams of the voices calling me about once a week, and eventually they faded away. But never again did I go into the attic in my dreams. Now that I am older, I believe that this was my first out-of-body experience.

—*Danyel Boone,*
Rochester, N.Y.

Where Was the Tunnel and the Light?

Twenty-some years ago, I was in a very abusive relationship. After a year of daily beatings and many unsuccessful attempts to leave the situation, I saw no other way out: I swallowed 60 sleeping pills. I took them at work after everybody else had left. I figured that I could make it to the subway, then fall asleep during the commute, and no one would take notice until the very last stop.

My plans were disrupted. My lover and abuser picked me up at work. When we got to the subway, I was already moving very slowly and my speech was blurred. He thought I was drunk. When we got off, he knew something was very wrong. He dragged me home, and finally threatened me into telling what I had done.

"Do you honestly think I'm going to call an ambulance and save your f— life?" he yelled at me.

"I don't care," I vaguely remember responding.

He called 911 anyhow, dragged me down the four flights of our apartment building and made me walk up and down the sidewalk. "You can't go to sleep!" he kept yelling at me.

In the ambulance someone kept asking me questions and I begged, "Just let me go to sleep!" I felt as though I was experiencing a very high dose of nitrous oxide and had never felt more wonderful in my life.

Then came the fog. I wandered around in this fog for what seemed an eternity. Spirits approached me from all sides. Some I recognized as friends who were still alive. Some I recognized as people who were dead. Many I did not recognize at all. I do not remember what they had to say, but overall I felt as though the general message was that I was not done on the earthly plane.

When I woke up, I was in a hospital room. The girl in the bed next to me gasped, "It's about time! You drove me nuts all night with your talking to all kinds of invisible people!"

I was back. For years thereafter, whenever I felt safe enough to share this experience with someone, I got this warm feeling. If it hadn't been for the danger involved—I no longer wanted to die—I would have tried to bring that experience back.

The only thing that confused me was the near-death description of other people. I never saw a light or a tunnel. Did I really experience near death?

Years later I read a book called *The Other Side and Back*, by Sylvia Browne, a psychic who often appears on TV. In one of her chapters she describes what happens to suicides. And there it was—the fog. Sylvia calls it the gray area. A suicide is met on the other side by spirits who successfully made the transition and by those who are still confused. Either side tries to pull you their way. At last, I understood what I had gone through.

—Heidi Kaminski,
Tecumseh, Mich.

Through the Looking Glass

Out-of-body experiences tend to be a rare thing. But when they do happen they sure pack a wallop. Surprise, fear, and awe are just some of the emotions one experiences.

I had been ill throughout 1988, and my doctors weren't sure what was wrong with me. By December, I had lost 90 pounds and chunks of hair were coming off in my hand. I slept all day but never very well. I was confident it was either cancer or a sickness I had created in my mind.

I spent all of December 15 asleep. I'd wake every now and then to try to eat. I kept getting this "light" feeling, like all my bones were loose. I felt like I could slip out of my body at any moment and was fairly sure I would die that night.

Three a.m. rolled around and I found that I had not died. Instead, I was hungry. The rest of the household was asleep and I decided not to bother them while I went to the kitchen for some food.

There's a sliding-glass door near the kitchen that leads to a patio where my two dogs live. I hadn't seen them for days and had a sudden urge to go outside and play with them. I took one step toward the glass door and suddenly found myself outside. I'd passed through the glass without opening it, like Alice stepping through the Looking Glass into Wonderland.

My oldest dog started growling. I must have frightened her, because she had never growled at me before. I reached down and petted her, scratched behind her ears, and cuddled her a bit. She calmed down a bit and flattened her ears, though she was still a bit startled. My other dog never came out of her house; she was simply too scared. After several minutes it started getting cold, so I stepped back inside the same way I went out—through the glass itself.

When I got back to my room, I found my body still asleep in bed. I just stood there, watching my emaciated self sleep. I started to wonder: Was I truly dead, or did I just get loose for a while? Then my body shifted in its sleep. Not dead: always a good sign. I got back into bed and cuddled up next to myself and closed my eyes.

When morning came, I was able to get out of bed, body and soul reconnected. The first thing I did was step out onto the patio to check on my pets. My oldest dog's reaction was one of fright—she took a step back, hackles raised. While I reassured her that I wasn't a ghost, she reassured me that what had happened wasn't a dream.

My illness was diagnosed later that week and the prescribed medication had me up and about in less than a month. I was never entirely sure if the illness had caused the incident, but I haven't had an experience like it since. Neither have my dogs.

—*Stephanie Luna,*
Montebello, Calif.

I Saw "the Light"

In February 2001, I came down with a chest cold, which progressed quickly to bronchitis, then pneumonia. I had a history of respiratory illness, and did not worry too much about recovering and returning to work sooner rather than later. I was mistaken.

I have had pneumonia before, in fact many times before, so I knew what the next several weeks would entail. However, this particular illness was different. I quickly succumbed to it, becoming really, really sick within the course of two weeks. I was almost bedridden, only getting washed and dressed to go to the doctor's office and back home. I could barely do that.

March 10, 2001, started out as the days before it, with coughing, expectorating, utter fatigue, and almost despair. I had been really sick before, but this was like nothing I had ever experienced. I was beginning to wonder if I would make it—would I survive this episode? This Saturday afternoon, I lay down on my bed, staring out the window at the blue sky and tree branches in between, when I began to doze off to sleep, something I did with great regularity those days.

I could feel my body relax. I could feel my respiration rate slow considerably. I was in a light sleep one minute, a deep sleep the next, and then something happened. My body felt much lighter, as if I was floating on water or in the air! I saw a circular light coming toward me—or was I moving toward it? I wasn't sure. Instantly, I knew what it was, and what was happening . . . I was moving into "the light" I had heard about. I was dying.

It was clear to me, as the light and I moved closer to one another. I said to myself, "I am not ready to go. I am not ready to go." It was absolutely peaceful, no pain, absolutely tranquil, as the very strong pull toward the light progressed.

I could then hear my mother calling me. "Hi, Mark," she said in her Danish accent.

I continued to say, "I am not ready to go." I could feel myself resisting this force. I was not dreaming.

Suddenly, I could feel my lungs fill with air, and from my deep sleep or whatever I had just experienced, I awoke very startled and unnerved. These uneasy feelings remained with me for the next several days.

I did not fear death before March 10, nor do I now, some six months later. I still have respiratory illnesses, and my doctors do not know exactly what my prognosis is. Whatever does happen, I know that the next time I see "the light," I will go . . . that is, if I am ready.

—Mark K. Bayless,
Berkeley, Calif.

Little Drummer Boy

Long before I read Moody, Muldoon, Myers, or Crookall, or heard of such things as OOBEs, NDEs, or astral projection, I had an out-of-body experience.

"The Little Drummer Boy" is hardly my favorite Christmas song, but hearing it always takes me back to that December day in 1974. I was an anxious eighth-grader in Coopersville, Michigan, who was about to play the snare drum solo in the junior high band's rendition of that song. Clutching drumsticks in cold, sweaty, trembling palms, I watched apprehensively as the conductor raised her baton and signaled me to begin playing.

Suddenly I realized I was calmly watching the performance from the audience. My body continued pa-rum-pa-pum-pumming on the stage while "I" sat as a spectator in the gymnasium bleachers. Near the end of the performance, I became aware of being back in my body on stage in the percussion section.

This did not seem strange to me at the time. I was just grateful to have made it through the entire song.

It was not until years later that I thought of it as an anxiety-induced out-of-body experience.

To this day I cannot say with certainty whether what happened to me was an entirely internal, defensive dissociative experience, or if my consciousness actually left my body in an instance of what researchers have termed "somatic dissociation." The former explanation seems hardly sufficient to account for the shift in perspective that allowed me to see my own and other band members' faces and the conductor's back as if from a distance.

Whichever the case, the experience enabled me to survive a potentially debilitating episode of stage fright. In time the memory of it also deepened my interest in the dissociation of consciousness and my conviction that consciousness and personality can exist beyond the confines of the physical body.

—*Michael K. Kivinen,*
Wyoming, Mich.

My Near-Death Experience

A few years ago, I had a near-death experience. I have sleep apnea, which means that sometimes during my sleep I stop breathing. One night I dreamed that I was aboard a submarine that was filling up with water. Soon I was holding my breath and looking for a means of escape. I felt a few seconds of fear that soon gave way to a darkness filled with millions of stars, which amazed me. I remember thinking: *This is beautiful; I could get used to this.*

As I continued what I felt to be an upward and forward movement, I could see that I was heading for a small circle of light. The closer I got, the bigger the circle became, and I could see the beginning of a place taking shape. Finally I arrived in a big beautiful room. It was brilliant with color, with large marble pillars that seemed to go all the way up to infinity. This room seemed to be a lobby of sorts that had rooms going off in all directions, but the doors were covered with thick draperies.

I didn't see anyone, but rather felt and heard them telling me that I had to go back; it was not my time to cross over. I responded by saying that I was not ready to leave, I wanted to see more. Again, more sternly, I was told I had to go back to my body. True to my nature, I insisted on staying—I wasn't ready to leave. I felt light, free of pain and worry, and so incredibly loved. I felt as if I was finally home. I forgot my life and my family. All I knew was that I wanted to stay where I was.

Finally I was told that if I didn't go back to my body right away, I would never be able to go back. I remember responding that I didn't care; I wanted to stay. But before I could get that statement out I felt as if there was a rope pulling me backwards rapidly. All of a sudden, I fell—literally—back into my body.

I was fully awake, oriented, and angry that I was back in my body. I even tried holding my breath, hoping that I would be able to leave my body and go back to that wonderful place.

No longer am I afraid to cross over. I know where I am going, and it is just a transition from earth walker to spirit walker. I often wondered why I was given this gift of sight into the spirit world. Slowly the reason was given to me.

I am a registered nurse, and my area of practice is mental health. After my experience, I began to get clients who were in the last stages of various terminal illnesses. When the time was right, I was able to share my near-death experience with these clients and their families. It seemed to give them a sense of peace. They didn't struggle so when their angel came for them. The loved ones left behind felt confident they would see them again, and many have called to share with me the fact that they can still feel their loved ones checking in from time to time.

Another benefit I got from my NDE was that my psychic gift got stronger, and I am able to help a lot of other people with that gift. Even though my time on the other side was brief, the life-changing event will carry me through until it is my time to cross over, and this time to stay!

—Linda Dix,
Toledo, Ohio

I Was with Him

I was four years old when my father died and I knew before I was told—because I spoke with him.

Mother received a telephone call from Dad's employers telling her Dad was on his way home and extremely ill. Mom called an ambulance and whisked me off to a neighbor's house. She returned home to wait for Dad and the ambulance.

When my father walked into the house, Mom knew something was wrong. His eyes were bloodshot and he complained of a terrible headache. He went into the bathroom and, using the toilet as a seat, he sat down beside the sink. He wet a folded washcloth and pressed it against his eyes and forehead.

I walked into the bathroom and stood silently watching my father. He must have sensed my presence because he raised his head and looked at me. I'll never forget his eyes—blood-red with pain showing within their depths. I felt them burning.

"Daddy . . . "

He looked at me with a deep, loving look and said, "It's all right, Honey. Everything will be all right."

After that, memory fails me. I seemed to fade into the background. I have no recall of how I arrived or how I returned to the neighbor's house. The sense of fading into the background after having spoken with my father remains with me today.

I spent the night with the neighbor, who was a friend of my mother's. I remember waking during the night, frightened. I saw a clock that appeared to read 1:15 and I cried, "My daddy's dead!"

Mary soothed me back to sleep.

The next day when Mary brought me back to our house, I told my mother, aunt, and grandmother that my daddy was dead. I did not think they knew.

Mom and I never talked about that time. Mom was devastated and I was too young to understand. I knew that talking about Dad made Mom cry.

Years later while Mom and I were spending an evening together I started telling her about talking with Dad the day he died.

Mom stared at me with a puzzled look on her face until I stopped talking.

"You couldn't have spoken with your father and you couldn't have seen him. You were not there."

"Yes, Mom, I was there. I walked into the bathroom where he was sitting. He was holding a white washcloth to his forehead. When he looked at me his eyes were bloodshot. They were burning him badly."

Again, Mom told me I could not have been there. "You were at Mary's house. She was keeping you away."

I became frustrated with Mom and argued that I had indeed been there. I described the clothing Dad was wearing and what he was doing. I told her what Dad said to me and explained how I always had the sensation of backing up and fading into the wall.

Mom said, "You had an out-of-body experience, then. There was no way you could have left Mary's house because you couldn't reach the locks on the doors. And there was not enough time for you to have come in and gone back out . . . the ambulance arrived and we got in it and left. You were not there physically. That probably explains the feeling of fading backwards."

"Mom, Dad died at 1:15 in the morning, didn't he?"

"Why?"

"I woke up and saw a clock that read 1:15 and I started crying and told Mary my daddy was dead."

"He died at 12:15. You didn't see the two. Honey, you couldn't tell time when you were four years old."

It took my mother telling me to convince me that I had that experience. I spent my life until then believing I had been with my dad just before he died when in fact my physical being was separated from him by walls and time.

—*Jo Davis,*
Arcadia, Mo.

It's Not Your Time

It had been a rough night shift at Boeing for me. As I sat on the bus at Fourth Avenue and Pike Street in Seattle, the old bus driver questioned me about my whereabouts for the past four nights. I said he would not believe me if I told him, but he insisted. "Try me!"

My story drew the attention of others as they heard me tell him I had been to Hell and back in those four days.

I had fallen ill, and my doctor, Jean Bourdeau, had taken lab tests which revealed I had meningitis. After discussing with three other doctors whether or not to tell me, he informed me I had less than 24 hours to live. I checked into Seattle General Hospital for my last hours on earth.

Upon checking into the hospital, I was assigned to a special room: no one in, no one out. The three doctors stuck tubes into my arms to feed me. They even used a long hose, shoved down my nose, to wash my stomach out with sudsy water. Having worked me over, Dr. Bourdeau then came to me, and we talked for a long time. He spoke about the many times he had seen me in the past, how he had appreciated things I had done, and then he fell quiet.

"You have only a few hours left to live," he said. He knew that I had no family, no relatives, and here, with only a few hours left to live, he tried his best to say goodbye without hurting me. He then mixed three different antibiotics and shot them directly into my vein.

We shook hands, and he told me to pray as that was all that was left. They had done all they could for me medically. He started to leave, turned around and said, "If you are still here, we will take it from there."

Everyone on the bus was listening more closely now. I explained that within an hour, I was gone. I realized that I was no longer in my body but elsewhere, and it was then I was shown Hell as it was, but I went on past it, headed toward a beautiful city in full deep color. I saw former friends and relatives who had been dead for years. Suddenly, someone behind me said, "You cannot go on. It is not your time; you have to go back."

I turned around and there stood a young friend I knew from the Army Tank Corps. I refused to go back, but somehow, he sent me to my body in the hospital.

A young Chinese woman was working me over physically. As I opened my eyes, she said, "So, you are back. I am Dr. Wong."

I spoke aloud with her. She was in a street dress, and I found it impossible to believe she was a doctor.

The nurse who guarded the door to my room to prevent people entering came in to see to whom I was speaking. She could hear someone walking around, but only me talking. When the nurse asked me where the person was, I told her she was at the nightstand, but as we looked, no one was there. The nurse searched everywhere, but there was no Dr. Wong to be seen.

My temperature was normal and the pain gone. The nurse checked me over, and we both looked at the clock. My 24 hours were now gone and I was still alive.

Bourdeau called it a miracle, as did the other doctors who worked on me. I had gone to Hell and seen things no living person has seen, and returned to tell about it.

The bus driver was now totally engrossed in my experience, as were the other passengers who listened. I told them I later received a letter from a friend who had learned that the night the Army Tank Captain had told me to go back, he had accidentally shot himself to death while cleaning his weapon. He was not alive when I saw him on the other side.

Now I understand things in a different way. We on earth are judges of our own; however, the final judges are on the other side of life's curtains, and their laws are different from those we face on earth. If more knew our lives on earth are recorded on the other side, we may think twice before breaking their laws. Once broken, we have to pay for them in different ways still unknown to man himself.

It only takes a half-second for one to pass from this life to Hell or Heaven, and few, if any, return to tell about it. I may have been one of the more fortunate ones for having experienced the journey beyond reason.

—*Leon Thompson,*
Kent, Wash.

5

Haunted Places

I make no claim to being especially sensitive to psychic matters, but certain locations have an uncanny aura strong enough that even a spiritually dense person like me can pick up on it.

Back when I was a single apartment-dweller, I was often called upon by friends and family to housesit. I was perfectly comfortable in most places, but there were a couple houses that gave me the creeps. Nothing dramatic ever happened; I just couldn't shake the feeling that I wasn't alone.

Cases of haunted houses (and other buildings) reported to FATE go way beyond anything most of us will experience. In some, unexplained phenomena may continue for years or decades. Research into the history of the house and its former residents may reveal clues regarding the reason for the haunting and the identity of the spirits involved. Sometimes this information can lead to the haunting's resolution; in other cases, the resident ghosts are benign or even helpful.

In recent years, ghost hunting has become an enormously popular activity. Legions of hobbyists now swarm through haunted locations with cameras, audio recorders, and EMF meters hoping to collect evidence of spirits. However, the testimony of those who have lived with a haunting remains the best evidence.

Who's Here?

Who's here? I thought to myself.

It was November 1980, and I was unpacking dishes in the kitchen of our new house when I thought I heard adult voices in the living room. Knowing my three children and I were alone in the house, I wondered who the kids had let in. I went into the living room and found the room empty.

All three of my kids were in their respective rooms, with no adults in sight. I must have heard noises of adults talking from outside the house, I concluded. The neighboring houses were closer to my new home than any other houses I had lived in recently. Maybe the neighbors were in their yards, and their voices sounded like they were in our house.

Several times the next day, I again thought I heard a man and a woman talking in my house. When I went to find where the voices were coming from, I could never figure it out. The voices would stop. I looked outside to see if I could see anyone, but no one was there.

We had just moved in and I was not yet used to the noises in my new house, I told myself.

As most parents do, every night just before I went to bed, I always checked to make sure my children Stacy (age 12), Josh (age 4), and Brian (age 2) were in bed and covered. The second night we were in the house, I went to check on the kids. They were all asleep, but when I went to pull up the covers on Josh, I saw a very large butcher knife lying under his neck. Horrified, I lifted his head and neck up and removed the knife. It looked as if he had put the knife under his pillow and it had worked its way out from under the pillow to just under his neck. He did not have any cuts on him, but I wondered what might have happened to him later during the night if I had not removed the knife.

The next morning I asked Josh why he had put the knife under his pillow, but he would not respond. My instincts told me he put the knife under his pillow to protect himself—but from what or whom?

The third day in the house, I came home from work to fix myself lunch. Having earlier driven Stacy to school and Josh and Brian to the babysitter's, I knew I was alone in the house. I ran upstairs to Stacy's bedroom to grab some papers I had left in her room, and then came downstairs and opened the refrigerator to see what I could find for lunch.

Suddenly, someone stomped loudly across the floor in Stacy's room, directly above the kitchen. This was not a "someone-is-walking-across-the-floor" noise, but a loud, "I-am-stomping-as-loudly-as-I-can-to-make-sure-that-you-can-hear-me-stomping!" noise.

Shaken, I decided that I did not need lunch after all that day and went back to work hungry.

That evening, I gathered my children and my ex-husband, who had been helping us move in, and asked, "Has anyone heard or seen anything unusual about this house?"

Stacy started by saying, "I hear people's voices and coughing all the time. When I go and look, no one is there."

Craig, my ex-husband, told of when he was staying at the house late to help unpack and was the only one awake. He was sure he had heard Stacy walk down the stairs from her bedroom, through the living room, dining room, and hallway, and then downstairs to the basement. Wondering what she would be doing up at that hour, he had followed what he had thought were her footsteps. When he had arrived at the basement stairs, the hook-and-eye closure was locked. Puzzled, he had reasoned that the hook must have swung up and locked itself. When he had opened the basement door, he saw that no lights were on. He had been so convinced that he had heard her go downstairs that he had gone and checked the basement. She had not been there. He had gone back upstairs and found her asleep in her bed.

Josh would not answer our questions.

Brian said he had been talking to Sue and Dan, who, he said, "live in our attic." He said he liked to talk to his new friends.

Since the director of the local School of Metaphysics was a friend of mine, I asked her to come over and give me advice. What should one do about living in an apparently haunted house?

The director told me that people on the physical plane were stronger than were those on the astral plane. If I ordered the ghosts out of my house, they would have to leave.

I stood in the middle of my living room floor and loudly said, "I bought this house for my kids and me to live in. I do not want anyone else to live here with us. I want you to move out!"

I heard no voices in the house after that. A couple of days later, however, Stacy told me that she had heard voices again.

Again, I ordered the ghosts to leave. That was the last any of us heard the voices.

We lived in that house for four years. When we moved out and I was walking down the stairs from Stacy's bedroom, I strongly felt that the ghosts were moving back in. I felt their anger and their impatience to have me leave. The feeling was so strong that I grabbed the railing to the stairs and held on tightly, feeling as if someone might push me down the stairs.

Years later, I called the person who then lived in my old house. I coincidentally found her number in the phone book when I was looking up my husband's name to see if it was listed in the book correctly. Directly under my husband's name was the name and phone number of the woman who was living in my old house.

I held my breath and made the call. I remember the conversation clearly. I said, "Hello, this is Diane Lawson. I used to live in your house from 1980 until 1984. I was wondering if you have noticed anything unusual about your house?"

There was a long pause. She said, "I am so glad you called. My children and I are living with ghosts. It is against my religion and I don't have anyone to talk to about it."

She went on to tell me that she and her children were experiencing exactly what my children and I had gone through. She also said that when she was on the computer, she would feel the ghosts' presences and see someone out of the corner of her eye. When she would turn to look, there would be nothing there. She assured me that it was not her imagination. She felt certain ghosts were near her.

Talking to the new owner made me want to find out if a Sue and a Dan had ever lived in the house, as two-year-old Brian had believed years before. My husband and I went to the public library and looked at many city directories between 1903 and 1980. We found that two women named Susan had lived in that house. We also found a man named Dan who had the same unusual last name as one of the Susans and may have been related to her.

I do not know who was in the house when we lived there, but I do know that whoever they were, they made their presences known to eight people, independently of one another, over a 20-year period.

—*Diane Lawson,*
Topeka, Kans.

True Believers

Maybe ghosts know who believes and who doesn't, and that's why my son, Joshua Pleasnick, and I seem to attract them like magnets. After living in all but one house where we have had ghostly encounters, we are truly firm believers.

It all started in 1989, when Joshua turned eight and we moved to a very rural community in an old farmhouse built in 1865. The house needed much refurbishing so walls were torn down, carpets removed, and floors stripped. Many rooms looked like a demilitarized zone and were off limits due to dangerous nails and metal strips lying around.

One day Joshua walked by the doorway of a room we were working on. As he looked in he saw a man in bib overalls feeding chickens. The man was shorter than Joshua's father, James Pleasnick. He was balding, with a big potbelly, and wore a plaid shirt and old shoes. He was tossing the chickens some sort of grain.

Joshua ran outside, quite shaken. When he told James and me the story, we brushed it off. We knew that he wanted to get chickens and thought he had just come up with a creative way to get us to give in.

Shortly after that we were at a local function where I mentioned it to the pastor and his wife. A nearby "old-timer" overheard the conversation and said the person I described sounded exactly like the brother of the people that had first owned the house we lived in. She named him, and went on to say that every winter the wife's brothers (there were 13 of them) came to live with her family in the house we now owned. The brothers worked out west during the summer and came back to the Midwest every winter. The family always had chickens roaming the yard and would bring them into the parlor during the winter months.

She described the house as it was back in the 1920s to early '50s when the brothers were there. The portion of the house she described as the parlor was exactly where Joshua saw the man feeding the chickens.

Many years later we moved to another old house, this one a Victorian from the 1890s. Joshua's room was at the top of the stairs, just past another room we had yet to use.

Joshua came home from school one day and ran up the stairs to his room. At the top of the stairs, the spare room's door was open and he saw a woman bent down wearing all black and appearing to be scrubbing the floor.

"Hi Mom!" he yelled, and went into his room. He never heard a reply, and started to think about how odd it was that I was wearing all black and scrubbing the floor, so he went back to look again. This time, no one was there.

Joshua came downstairs to get a snack just as I walked in the back door. He asked me if I had just been upstairs, and then looked at my clothes, asking how I changed so fast. After I told him I had just gotten home from work, he told me what had happened to him.

A week or so later I went to town to pick up an order at a catalog store. After I gave the woman my address, she said, "Oh, I used to live there! Is it still haunted?"

She proceeded to describe the same woman my son had seen, telling me she had seen her also scrubbing floors and crying. She had checked the history of the house and found that there was a woman who had lived there around the early 1900s who had lost her young husband, but she could never discover how he died.

After my son grew up and moved out on his own, I bought my own house. When I first came to look at the house I was met by the owner. He told me that he had lost his wife recently and needed to move away, thus he wanted out fast. I was thrilled to buy the house but knew I would want to make some cosmetic changes.

Before the closing I mentioned the house to a co-worker as well as the name of the man I was buying it from. She stated that that name had just appeared in the obituaries only a short time ago.

I looked in the paper and found that the owner's wife had died only two days before I'd looked at the house, and that she hadn't even been buried yet when I put in my offer to purchase. In talking with the neighbors I found out she had died in what was to be my bedroom.

Immediately after closing on the house I went alone to clean and paint before I moved in my things that weekend. As I stood in front of the kitchen counter and began to wash out the cabinets, I talked out loud to my dog about all the changes I would make to the house to make it my own. Suddenly I was pushed in the small of my back, and my hips hit the countertop edge as my shoulders arched backwards. Immediately I knew it was Linda, the wife of the man I had bought the house from. I was told she had never wanted to leave the house, though he had been trying to get her to move for years.

Again I began to speak out loud, telling Linda of all I went through to get the house, how I was on my own and needed to be there. I expressed that I would take care of the home, but she could not stay. I have never had any other incidents and feel I was able to help put her to rest.

My son recently bought his own house and so far has had no ghostly encounters, but when and if they occur in the future, neither he nor I will be surprised. We have become true believers.

—Marie Boyum,
Racine, Wis.

My Haunted Victorian Home

It was the fall of 1993. My husband Gary and I had been looking for a new home in a different community for about two years. We had just made a three-and-a-half hour drive to see what we hoped would be our new residence.

The house was a huge old Victorian residence with other buildings on the property. Quite impressive, even though it was in fixer-upper state.

We thoroughly combed through the house and the other buildings as well. The realtors were nice and even allowed us to stay and continue to look and discuss the property while they went back to their office.

As we went back downstairs, I noticed a square board leaning against a doorway. As I bent over to pick it up, a cold breeze blew across the back of my neck. I must have straightened up with a strange look on my face. Gary asked what the problem was, so I told him. It was then that we both noticed that the square board was a type of Ouija board. We looked at each other and laughed. Were we about to buy a haunted house?

We were sure this was the right house for us. The price was right, the terms were right. And so it was that we acquired our new home.

We moved in on Halloween night. We were exhausted after two days of packing and moving ourselves. We threw our mattress on the dining room floor and collapsed to sleep for a while.

I was shaken awake in the middle of the night by a woman who seemed very anxious to have me come with her. (I have been having psychic experiences since I was about four years old and have learned to take them as no more disturbing than a phone call.) I was too tired to follow her and turned over and went back to sleep.

In the morning, I told Gary what had transpired. He felt I probably should have gone with her. My reply was that if it was important, she'd be back. Unfortunately, she never came back to show me what was so important.

I know there are those who would attribute both these incidents to imagination, especially the one on the night of our arrival. We were shortly to get confirmation that we were not so alone in the house.

A couple months passed and Gary got a job at a foundry, working 12-hour shifts. That left me in the house alone quite a bit, especially at night.

The first step on our stairs would creak under pressure of someone's weight, but never by itself. There were numerous nights that I would hear that step creak as if someone was climbing the stairs. I thought I was just hearing things until one night when my husband was home and he heard it too.

This was further confirmed in later months when we had some friends staying with us. One morning, my friend Deb asked my husband if he had gotten home early. She had heard the front door opening, footsteps coming down the hallways, and someone climbing the stairs. She was confused, however, because she heard the same sequence of events at the normal time of my husband's return from work.

Gary laughed and told her that it must have been the resident ghost.

That was far from being the end of the strange events here. It didn't take us long to figure out that the house held more than one ghost.

One day I noticed a man out in front of our house taking pictures. I went down and asked him if I could help him. He introduced himself and told me that as a boy he had visited the house often. His grandmother and grandfather had owned the house. He filled me in on parts of the family and house history, explaining that the downstairs hadn't been used since his grandfather's death in 1936.

He then proceeded to tell me that once when he had come to stay, after his grandfather's death, he had been allowed to stay in his grandfather's bedroom downstairs. During the night, his grandfather had come to visit him. Of course, none of the adults had believed him, but he assured me that even now, as an adult of some years, he knew what he had experienced that night was real.

To me, this gave an explanation to that breeze across the back of my neck on our first visit to the house and also to the footsteps and stair-climbing my friend Deb had reported.

I had begun to research the history of the house to see if I could find out anything else about the building or its occupants over the years. In the process of my search, I ran across some pictures of Alice Faine, the last resident of the house prior to our purchase. Imagine my shock and surprise when I recognized the woman who had awakened me on my first night in the house!

More incidents have happened over the years, both to myself and others, that only confirm that not only is the house haunted, but it has an upstairs ghost, Alice, and a downstairs ghost, her father.

One other thing, that we found out later, says it all. When I told the realtors that I believed the house was haunted, one of them, without even cracking a smile, told us that that might explain what happened to the previous purchaser. He explained that a man had put down a $1,500 deposit on the house in June and had even begun work on it. When it came time for the closing, the man never showed up. He also never called or tried to get his deposit back. Could he have been chased from the house by Alice's father, or even by Alice herself?

—*Samantha Herron,*
New Straitsville, Ohio

A True Ghost Story

What is the true appearance of a ghost? A chance encounter with the spectral world put that question to rest when our family experienced a ghost story of our own.

It was October 1975, and we were hoping to find a suitable house to rent in Pittsburgh, Pennsylvania, with little success. Finally, after an exhaustive search, we came upon a lovely old farmhouse that was listed for rent. Amazed at our good fortune, we immediately contacted the realtor and soon reached an agreement. It never occurred to us to ask if we would be the only residents. That turned out to be our first mistake.

We had scarcely settled in when the original tenant decided to make his presence known. All too soon, we awoke to the fact that the house was haunted . . . a fact the real estate agent had neglected to mention.

Our ghostly introduction took place as we entertained a few close friends for a housewarming party. One of our guests was an elderly minister who had been our special friend for many years. He was reputed to possess psychic powers and had helped cleanse houses of negative energy.

As the party progressed, the reverend detached himself from the guests and motioned me aside for a quiet talk.

"I like your new house," he began, "but I couldn't help wondering if you feel comfortable living here."

"Of course we do! But why do you ask?"

He gave me a cryptic smile. "I just saw a young man walk across the kitchen floor who was not one of your guests!"

While Reverend Nathaniel was the first to encounter our ghost, he was not the last. The ghost made his next appearance one rainy afternoon as my two-year-old son Patrick was riding his tricycle around the house making loud motor sounds. Suddenly, I became aware of absolute silence, and my son was nowhere to be seen. I found him in the hallway at the foot of the stairs, staring up toward the bedrooms.

He turned to me and whispered, "Mommy, a man went into that bedroom!" He pointed upward in stunned silence.

I hurried upstairs, calling loudly, "You there, come out! I've called the police!" But a check showed only empty bedrooms.

My teenage daughter Tammy occupied the room the ghost had entered, so she became the next person to question.

"Mom," she said, "I know there's a ghost here. I haven't seen him, but he rattles the blinds and walks about, wanting to be noticed! He's a gentle ghost. Harmless. I'm not afraid!"

The third spirit encounter involved another two-year-old boy who came with his mom for a visit. I had invited my recently widowed friend Carole to share our home. I needed a live-in babysitter so I could begin working a night shift at the post office. She seemed the perfect candidate.

Carole readily agreed to the invitation. We were pleased to note how well our boys played together. It seemed nothing could go wrong. But then it did: enter our resident ghost.

Carole stayed that first night, but the following morning I found a frightened young woman waiting impatiently for my return. She was already packed.

"I'm sorry, the deal is off!" she told me. "You said nothing about having a ghost!"

"What are you talking about? What happened?" I tried to feign innocence but my heart went down to my toes.

"In the middle of the night, my son shook me awake, pointed to the empty hallway and asked me, 'Mommy, who is that man standing there?' There wasn't anyone there, but he kept that up all night long. It was a night I'll never forget, though I wish to God I could! I'm sorry, I just can't stay here. You'll have to find someone else."

I was beginning to feel left out of the ghost equation. "I can't deal with something I can't see," I pleaded. "I want to help you, but you have to let me know what you want!"

To my surprise the ghost quickly provided an answer. One night soon after, we experienced a fierce thunderstorm. As the house rattled and groaned, there came a different sound from the entrance to Tammy's room, similar to someone repeatedly opening and closing the door. It was obviously intended to get someone's attention, and it did.

As a flash of lightning illuminated the hallway, I saw him: a young man in his late teens or early 20s with blond hair in a military style crew-cut. He was wearing a light green T-shirt with a narrow, white-edged collar. He floated down the hall at a rapid speed, his form cloaked in a soft green light. But it was his face that caught my attention. There was a sadness and frustration edged in every line.

In my mind, I heard the words: *Where is my family? Who are these people living in our house?* Then he faded into the wall and was gone.

He was reaching out to me for help and I decided I would do what I could to help. I began my search by paying a visit to our neighbor, a mailman. He and his family had lived there for over 20 years.

"Ed," I began gingerly, not wanting to be labeled a nut. "You've lived in this neighborhood a long while, haven't you?"

He nodded.

"Do you know of any folks who lived in our house, that died in the house?"

He scanned his memory. "Well, there was one man, an Italian. He had been sick a long time. But other than him, no one else."

I thanked him, and turned to leave, but he called me back. "Wait, there was one other one: a Polish family who lived in your house—it was their son! I remember hearing he had been killed in the war. A sad thing; he was quite young."

The pieces were beginning to fit together. I have heard that when someone dies unexpectedly, they don't know that they are dead, and are caught between two planes of existence. That could explain our ghost's confusion. I remembered a discussion in Bible school where a procedure was suggested that just might help.

I drove to a neighboring town to visit St. Mary's, our parish church. I knelt at the altar, lit a blessed candle, and fervently prayed for our ghost's release. As I looked up at the beautiful face of the Madonna, she seemed to smile reassurance.

Now I know what a ghost really looks like, and I have also learned that they don't return to frighten people, only to seek help. I've been asked if this haunting scared me. What mother witnessing the pain of a young person wouldn't want to reach out and offer comfort?

Happily, our haunting ceased, and the young man apparently moved on to find peace.

—*Alice McCormick,*
Boulder, Colo.

My Ghostly Pub

I did not believe in ghosts until I bought an old pub in England. After many years working in the computer industry, I wanted to try something completely different. Moving to England and becoming a publican qualifies. So in the spring of 1995 I closed up my computer software company, sold the house, and moved to the UK. The British Innkeepers Institute course was impossible to fail and, come the end of the summer, I found myself opening the Lord Admiral in the English Channel coastal town of Seaford, East Sussex. People flocked in to see the crazy Canadian running a British pub.

The square-shaped building had three floors and a basement. It was originally build in 1869 as an expansion to the hotel next door, but when the hotel was converted to apartments, the pub was sealed off and became a separate entity. It was a boxy kind of building with a lovely walled courtyard used as a beer garden in the summer, a restaurant/reception room on the next floor, and living quarters on the top floor. Seaford was an old smugglers' haunt and tunnels were said to run under the town. Bricked-off arches in the cellar looked rather mysterious. The floors creaked, the windows rattled, and the wind made strange noises as it rounded the corners late at night. It had to be haunted.

The first ghostly encounter was "the Vicar," a man dressed in black who usually sat in the back bar when it was empty. He would disappear as soon as you tried to focus on him, but his presence did not. Sometimes he could be felt as a cold spot in the hallway on the top floor.

A local woman had a chat with the Vicar after I got tired of his hanging around with an upset expression on his face. This medium was considered a witch by some of the locals. She claimed that the Vicar was a church deacon or something who had lived in a rectory on the site before the pub was built. It seems he was told that a pub would not be built here, only an extension to the hotel. He was not happy with the final outcome and would not rest until it was changed.

Good luck; you are in England, where there are more pubs than churches!

The second ghost was "the Lady Grey." She would slip into the back bar as the Vicar did when it was deserted. For some reason they never appeared together. I do not believe they came from the same era, so they did not know each other. She was the type of spirit you noticed out of the corner of your eye, always coming from the back entrance and moving silently and quickly behind your back. When you turned to see who was there, you could not so much see her as feel a female presence pass, dressed in a long grey dress.

One night we had a chimney fire in the fireplace in the back bar. After I made sure everyone was out and the fire brigade was on the way, one of the staff asked if I had gotten the woman in the grey dress out. She had seen the lady rush past the glass panel-door to the back of the pub. I searched, but of course found no one.

Why she was there and what she wanted was never made clear, nor were there any local records or stories of the woman. She seemed sad and I wished I could have helped her find peace.

One weekend, I left the pub in the care of my manager as we had decided to go on a short holiday. When we returned on the Sunday I was confronted by a pale-looking young man who declared that he would never stay alone in the pub overnight again. It appears that he was alone in a top-floor bedroom after closing up when he heard the sound of footsteps coming up the wooden stairs and then walking down the hall to stop in front of his door. Too terrified to move, he waited until the he heard them walk back along the hall and down the stairs. He then searched the building and found no one.

A few months later, I was alone one night in a different bedroom on the top floor and I too heard the clumping of steps on the bare wooden stairs. The steps slowly made their way down the hall to stop just outside my bedroom door. Surprisingly I had lost the ability to move and see who was there. After a short pause, the sound of steps retreated down the hall and then the stairs. There was one difference between my version and that of my manager's. He claimed to hear a man's footsteps, but I heard a woman in high heels. I too searched the building from top to bottom and found what I expected: nothing. The feeling from this one was not friendly at all.

One night after kicking out the last of the drinkers, cleaning up the bar, and closing up the till, I sat down to enjoy a nightcap in the back bar. I sat directly in front of the fireplace with the remains of the night's fire still glowing. It was comfortable and I was tired. To my back right was the glass-paneled door that came in from the back side of the bar. I heard this door open and close. I quickly looked that way and saw that it was the way it should be, closed and locked.

Hoping I was just hearing things, I concentrated on my drink and the fire again. I felt rather than saw a presence walk up beside me from the direction of the door. He stood at my right elbow and cleared his throat in a manner that made me feel I was taking all the room in front of the fireplace. Without thinking too much about it, I slid my chair over a couple of feet. It felt like the spirit sat down beside me in a nonexistent chair and disappeared. I felt no ill will or danger from this being, so I just finished my drink and went to bed.

The next day, wondering if I had really felt or heard anything, I went to the back bar and knew I was not alone.

Just as I was getting used to my spirit companions, another turned up in the form of a poltergeist. The bar ran straight down one side of the pub and ended in a curve with a few chairs around it. One slow night, I had just washed an ashtray, dried it, and placed it on the bar at the far end. When I removed my hand the thick crystal glass shattered into hundreds of pieces. It did not explode, just fractured like when a car windshield breaks. This happen right after I took my hand away.

Two days later an empty shot glass with a large solid bottom fractured and crumbled in the same area of the bar. After that a glass or ashtray would be found in pieces about once a week.

I was starting to accept the destructive sprite whenever it tried to startle me. One day I reached for a clean inverted beer glass to get a customer another drink. I grasped the bottom of the glass and as I raised it the top half shattered. I was left holding the intact bottom while the top was in pieces on the shelf. I am sure I heard a ghostly laugh.

Soon after that I sold the pub and went back into computers. After two years of owning a haunted pub, this seemed safer.

—*Rick Powell, North Vancouver,*
British Columbia, Canada

Are We Alone?

I live in a 160-year-old, two-story farmhouse. The house is surrounded by trees that provide plenty of shade against the hot days of summer. From all outward appearances, it's just a typical old farmhouse, but some of the things that have happened inside aren't so typical.

From reading the abstract, we learned that the single room upstairs was built as a wedding present for a couple named John and Abigail. Most of the eerie occurrences we have experienced happened in or around this room.

Sounds of someone walking up and down the stairs wake us up in the middle of the night. It sounds like they are wearing heavy work boots.

Under the stairway is a small closet. It's too small to be of any use, and it is empty. Muffled voices have often been heard coming from this area. You can never hear what is being said, but they are definitely voices.

One day, my stepdaughter was getting ready for work when she noticed our dog staring up at the top of the stairs. The strange smell of cigar smoke drifted down from upstairs. Needless to say, she left for work early that day.

Not everything that happens comes from the room upstairs. Several years ago, my son woke us in the middle of the night. He heard the cabinet drawers in the kitchen open and slam shut. He could hear the utensils rattling in the drawers. We searched the house and found nothing that would explain what caused the sounds. All the doors were still locked. Whatever it was, it didn't come from outside.

Every family member has experienced something here. Our children are all grown and out on their own, but they tell their experiences to anyone who will listen.

I didn't like to be alone in the house at night by myself, but when my husband had to spend some time in the hospital, I was forced to.

I had been at the hospital all day, and when I finally came home, it was late at night. My car lights barely lit the driveway because of the heavy fog that hovered like a cloud before me. I cursed myself for not leaving a light on before leaving that morning. The house was now dark as a tomb. I left my car, took a deep breath, and went into the house. It took a while, but I finally found the light switch.

I went through each room and turned on the lights. It had been a long day and I wanted to get some sleep. I wasn't brave enough to go in the bedroom, so I decided to sleep on the couch.

Just when I started to get comfortable, I heard the bedroom door upstairs slam three times. The sound was deafening in the quiet house. I slept in a chair until morning.

All of our kids have homes of their own now, and my husband and I live here alone. Or do we?

—*Loretta Kinley,*
Lafontaine, Ind.

6

Spirits Helping the Living

The files of FATE are filled with remarkable stories. Among the most amazing and inspiring of these are the type found in this chapter.

The accounts that follow suggest that spirits of the deceased not only appear to and communicate with the living but also, on rare occasions, provide assistance when it is most needed. Their unexpected help may simply offer encouragement or make life easier; in extreme cases it may rescue a loved one from a desperate or life-threatening situation.

We don't know how or why such extraordinary intervention occurs; we can only share these stories and wonder.

Insider Inspiration

During the recent wet April days, gray depression settled over me. I'd been a professional writer for several years. Now, everything about my life was moving slower and slower, especially my body. Could aging affect my writing, too?

I asked for a sign from the powers that be: Was I still supposed to be doing this? Maybe I had finished my writing career and should spend those hours in other activities. I swam or walked every day. I read and watched TV. I talked to friends and relatives on the phone or over a meal. Still no sign.

Was I asking for the impossible? I shopped for groceries and spent fun time in the nearby Goodwill store. My daughter and son-in-law sent me a ticket to visit them in California. If this was a sign, what did it mean? I missed the ongoing satisfaction that filled me when writing stories, poems, and articles. I spoke to my deceased parents and grandmother. Nothing.

I'd given up on receiving a sign, but I still wished for one. One day, I decided to sort through old papers. Sighing, I dragged a huge cardboard box from the hall closet. Letters, greeting cards, and other mementos from the last 40 years spilled from this box. What a mess! It was time to look through these souvenirs and keep only the ones that still had significance for me.

As I found several old letters from deceased relatives, I realized these were treasures to keep. I picked up one from my favorite Aunt Toni and started to read. She praised a story I'd written and sent her as she was dying of cancer. "Your writing is so good and meaningful! And I'm so proud of the way you're actually using your God-given talent. Keep it up."

Tears gathered in my heart and trickled from my eyes. My angel Aunt had come to inspire me. This was truly a sign!

—*Lucille R. Kraiman,*
Portland, Oreg.

The Lady in the Light

August 1961 had to be the worst month of my life. I had left my job at a Florida college and was taking summer classes at the University of Colorado in Boulder. I had no job for the fall, even though I'd registered with two teacher-placement agencies. Desperate, I drove to Denver to apply with the State Employment Bureau, which was located in a residential district. I parallel parked my car on a busy street under a "one-hour" sign and dashed upstairs to the Bureau's vast "help wanted" room.

After filling out the application form the busy clerk handed me, I waited on a bench, puzzling over my dream of the previous night. I was walking down a long, dark hall toward a light, in which stood a pudgy, middle-aged woman with a frown on her usually smiling face. It was

Miss Whitmer, my undergraduate English teacher and mentor at Ohio State University. We became friends, but over the years as I traveled the country, changed jobs, and ultimately wound up in Florida, we'd lost touch.

In my dream I stopped within a few feet of Miss Whitmer. "Move your car," she told me. Then I woke up.

The clerk called my name. "If you'd just come an hour earlier," she said. "I had an opening in Elko, Nevada."

I looked at my watch. My one-hour parking time was expiring, and I remembered Miss Whitmer's admonition.

"Excuse me," I said to the clerk. "I have to move my car. Please keep trying!"

I drove to a free space a block ahead and dashed back. The clerk was all smiles.

"I have a job for you. Dr. Wubben of Mesa College in Grand Junction, Colorado, just got a vacancy in the English Department. He's flying in tomorrow. Could you meet him at ten o'clock?"

I could, and I did, and I got the job. That afternoon I phoned the small private school in Columbus, Ohio, where Miss Whitmer used to teach in the summer. I wanted to thank her for her incredible "across-the-miles" advice, with the miraculous timing that changed my life.

The voice on the phone was full of regret. "I'm sorry. Miss Whitmer died ten years ago."

—*Lorraine Boschi,*
Grand Junction, Colo.

Unwanted Angel

After several failed marriages, Mother decided to give it one more try. My new stepfather was a political refugee from the USSR and an airplane pilot of no little expertise. Mother loved to fly so this seemed the perfect arrangement—to her, but not to me.

Her new husband was of the mind that I had been raised all wrong, and he was determined to "straighten me out." I was nearly grown at the time and not at all willing to be slapped around by a loudmouth with a thick European accent. Consequently, we did not get along; I didn't like him and told him so in no uncertain terms.

Mother and her new husband Al soon moved to a nearby city where he opened a flying school. I eventually married and in time my husband Carl and I became the parents of a daughter and son. Al was very fond of the kids, visiting as often as possible. Although he knew I didn't like him, he told me that he felt much closer to me than he ever had to his own children, whom he had "given up on."

Eventually Al became ill and unable to fly his beloved airplanes. One Sunday, he had Mother call to say he really wanted us to bring the kids to see him and that he wanted to talk to me. Mother sounded urgent, so we loaded the kids into the truck and drove the 50-some miles to the charming Victorian home that Al and Mother had restored.

I was appalled at Al's appearance; he really looked bad. Al told me that he had designated some of his "treasures" to be put away for the kids, and that he would always look after me, even after he was gone. Not long after that he passed over.

Mother sold the house and moved back home to be near me and my family. After some years she too became ill and passed over, as did my husband. The children had grown up and moved away, so I was left alone to cope with a land-grabbing neighbor who wanted my homeplace and vowed to stop at nothing to get it.

One evening, after a particularly trying day of battling the neighbor, I closed my eyes and said, "Please, if any of my guardian spirits are around, please, please tell me what to do."

I had expected a sign from my late husband or perhaps from one of my grandparents, who I felt were always nearby. But the voice I heard, a voice that could have come from someone in the same room, was not one of theirs.

Startled, I thought, *I know that voice, but who is it?* The voice had given the absolute perfect solution! Then it hit me.

"Al," I said, "is that you?" Right about then, an airplane buzzed the house, and I knew! After all those years, my stepfather was still with me.

From that time on, the land-grabber has, to all appearances, given up on his quest to get my home-place and is leaving me in peace. I feel that my stepfather and the rest of my guardian spirits are still hanging around, just in case things get out of hand.

—*Elizabeth Stutz Bishop,*
San Antonio, Tex.

Just Doing Her Job

When I began working the graveyard shift at a local nursing home, I found that many on the staff dreaded being alone on the east wing. They were even more fearful of a sitting room near the front of that hall. This room saw little care or attendance between 11:00 p.m. and 7:00 a.m.

Maybe it was the regular occurence of death associated with this particular wing. Maybe it was the facility's close proximity to a large cemetery that helped create a spine-tingling atmosphere. Maybe we really did, in fact, have a resident ghost.

There's no official story declaring the facility as "haunted," but anyone who ever worked third shift there will tell you there's no other explanation, myself included. Within a few days of the start of my job, I quickly understood what everyone was talking about.

Even when you were by yourself on the east wing, you were never alone. There was always a presence, like someone watching over your shoulder and supervising your duties. While maybe a bit astounding to the squeamish or unfamiliar employee, this presence quickly became a given fact. No one could have called it sinister.

The east sitting room was decorated with the early-20th-century belongings of the owner's grandmother, a woman who made nursing her life and inspired the medical careers of many loved ones. In this room, it was not unusual to see an indentation in the couch where someone had been sitting, though no one had been in there. More often than not, throw pillows would be rearranged, books or magazines opened or moved, and pictures that perpetually hung crooked would somehow straighten themselves. It was a regular occurence to hear beautiful music coming from the organ and to find the bench pulled out for a phantom player.

On a nightly basis, the call signals in the med room would light up, and though the residents in those rooms would deny having called us, most were usually in need of something. On more than one occasion, these so-called "ghost lights" were responsible for saving a life.

My co-workers and I have learned to live with our resident ghost. We're no longer frightened. In fact, we see her as a dear friend. Her presence is quite comforting, and we believe she's just doing what she loves: being a dedicated nurse and caring for her patients, even in the afterlife.

—*Stephanie Burtis,*
Springfield, Mo.

Spirit Nurse

My mother, Bessie Rayle, was a registered nurse and had worked as such up until her retirement. In June 1998, after her death, I was hospitalized and hooked up to an IV. I heard my name being called and woke up from a sound sleep. My mother was standing there in full nurse's uniform and told me to call the nurse to check my IV bag.

I glanced at the needle and noticed my blood backing up into the line, so I used the call button to summon the nurse. No one came, and my mother instructed me on safely removing the syringe, which I did.

When the nurse came, she was flustered and said that all the nurses were busy with an emergency patient and apologized. She checked the IV bag, which was empty, and told me that I had done a good job of removing the needle.

Another time, in January 1999, a student nurse who had been given instructions from a registered nurse injected a needle in the back of my hand. A short time later, my mother appeared to me, again in full uniform. She told me the needle was improperly injected and to call the nurse. I did so, and the nurse checked it and said it was fine. I could still see my mother and she pointed to my arm. I noticed a fine red line and showed the nurse. She immediately removed and replaced the needle, saying that it had been injected into the muscle in error and she would have a doctor inspect my arm.

I've been psychic all my life, so I believed in spirits already, but it was good to know that I had my own private nurse looking after me.

—Lois Algoe,
Euclid, Ohio

Communication from Beyond

It was 1975, two years after my mother died. She had always bought the children's school clothes in August and was especially devoted to my younger son. Now he was about to enter kindergarten.

One morning in August, as I crossed the family room to enter the kitchen, I saw a white envelope sticking out from under the VCR. I knew it had not been there before as I dust that unit weekly. Written on the outside, in my mother's handwriting, were the words: "For the boys' school clothes." Inside was $200 in cash.

I was stunned and couldn't believe my eyes. Trembling, I called my stepfather, who didn't believe me and came immediately to my house from work. He agreed the handwriting was my mother's and he had no explanation of how that envelope got under the VCR.

I was a bit hysterical over this, but I knew that my mother was making sure her beloved grandchildren would get new clothes for school.

—Lorrayne Salvin,
Westminster, Calif.

Her Daughter Came Back

Years ago, I found myself going to a complete stranger's house which was out of my way. Not knowing why I was going there or what I was supposed to say or do, I found myself asking the lady who answered the door if she would like to start a gardening club with me.

She said, "No thank you." She told me that her name was Barbara, and invited me in to chat. While we were chatting, I saw a figure in back of her chair. I was so surprised that Barbara asked me what was wrong, because I turned white as a ghost. (Believe me, if you saw a ghost, your face would turn white, too.)

Before I could think of anything to say, I found myself telling her, "Everything is fine and I'm okay. I want you to be happy." At the time, I wasn't even thinking of saying anything like that. Barbara asked me to describe the figure I saw. I told her that she was a young, blond woman, around 18 years of age and very pretty, wearing a pink dress. As there were no pictures in the living room, I couldn't have picked up the image from a picture.

I was so embarrassed, I didn't know what to do. I finally left. I found myself going over to her house a lot and we were best friends for 30 years, until she died.

Barbara told me, 20 years after we met, that she was about to commit suicide the day I first came to her house. The figure I saw was her daughter, who died of cancer six months earlier. She had been buried in her favorite pink dress.

Her daughter came back to save her!

—*Angeline Parmer,*
Universal City, Tex.

Uncle Hank

I was working as a children's librarian in the year 2000. I had been under strain, as I was the closest of Mom's four grown children and had taken it upon myself to see to her well-being after Dad died nine years earlier. This promise to look after my mother included regular long trips to visit her in Nashville, Indiana, taking her shopping and to doctor's and dental visits, cleaning her condo, and so forth.

Mom is an artist (mostly portraits and still lifes) and accustomed to walking every day, partying with her artist friends, and swimming at the YMCA twice a week. At 87 she was still an award-winning, working artist.

Mom's sister, my Aunt Nancy, and her brother, my Uncle Hank, had already passed on. Uncle Hank, who had at one time been a bass fiddle player with the Tommy Dorsey band in California, had succumbed to Parkinson's disease only a couple of years prior.

I had been getting more and more concerned about Mom because she was falling down on a weekly basis and her memory, which was normally pretty poor, was getting much worse. She just wasn't herself and I knew something was wrong with her. She was having what seemed to be neurological problems, weakness in the muscles, and trouble walking. I paused to wonder if she perhaps had Parkinson's as Uncle Hank had.

We had gone to her doctors twice. They had run some tests, but their attitude had been to pat Mom on the head and say, "That's just part of getting old."

I was livid! This was not my mother's normal state of mind and I knew she needed serious medical help. She was spiraling into a decline.

I was feeling helpless about the situation. It was preying on my heart and mind daily. So I prayed that God would use me as a go-between, a tool to help my mother get some help. She just was not demanding enough on her own behalf to get her point across with any force.

One day, I was standing behind the library circulation desk joking with my boss Jonnie and then turned around to face front again. There in broad daylight, in the middle of a well-lit public setting, stood the apparition of my dear Uncle Hank!

He looked thin and very stooped, as he had before he had died because he had neck curvature from osteoporosis. He appeared in good detail, though slightly transparent and not in color, yet a living presence nevertheless. There he stood, not two feet from the desk, smiling gently like a patron ready to check out a book! Then he was gone, vanished, leaving me feeling the awe and wonder that accompanies a visit from Heaven.

He had not spoken, but I knew right away what Uncle Hank had come to show me. No words were necessary; the message was clear. Mother had Parkinson's just like Hank, so I was convinced to go forward and insist on more medical attention.

After that, I was able to lean on the doctors, knowing my conviction was justified. They sent Mom to a neurologist. The new tests confirmed the bad news: she did have mid-stage Parkinson's.

The forthcoming treatment helped Mom get a lot of her strength back and although the disease still advances, she is 89 and fighting the good fight in an assisted-care facility with good staff to keep her safe.

Thank you Uncle Hank, for breaking the barrier between the two worlds to be your big sister Jeanne's guardian angel. You can visit me any time you wish.

—*Lisa Jo Brown,*
Amo, Ind.

Lightning

The ghost of my grandfather saved my life.

I graduated from high school surrounded by his family. Three uncles, an aunt, their families, and my grandmother stayed in my house with me, my brother, and my parents for the long weekend celebration.

My grandmother was delighted to see her oldest grandchild graduate from high school. My grandfather had passed away unexpectedly when I was only a year old. I was the only grandchild he met.

Lightning struck my house that night after my family left. The time was 11:11 p.m. *Crack!* I was startled awake. I sat up in bed, staring at the door. Silence echoed, loud after the loud noise. I got out of bed, wearing flannel pants and a T-shirt. I moved quietly, but I didn't know why.

My room was on the top floor at the end of the hall; at the other end was a closed door. The room was empty at the time. I didn't know that behind that door, the room was smoldering, and the attached attic was filling with smoke. I didn't know the roof was burning and the smoke alarms had been shorted out by the lightning.

I walked toward the door, intending to investigate the noise and the odd smell in the air. As I walked, a figure appeared at the top of the stairs between me and the fire. He was gray, indistinct. I knew him immediately as my grandfather.

"Don't go in there," he told me, though he didn't speak. We stared at each other. He didn't back down. Terrified, I ran back to my bedroom and dove under the covers. Eventually I fell back asleep.

Our dogs were restless and finally woke my parents. My father smelled smoke, called the fire department, and evacuated everyone.

By the time the flames were doused, the sun was rising. Most of the roof was gone. Every room reeked of smoke. Every surface in my bedroom was covered in a fine layer of oily soot. Our luggage had melted. My blackened school papers were blowing in the wind and catching on shrubbery.

Had I opened the door, I might have created a backdraft, consuming the room, the walls, the draperies, and myself. But the flames stayed contained in the attic and in the guest room, only starting to creep down the hall when the firefighters arrived. We all survived. I didn't open the door and spread the flames. My grandfather told me not to.

I keep a photograph of him on my bookshelf. I pester family for details of his life story. It's the least I can do.

—*Janine Peterson,*
Bethesda, Md.

7

Animal spirits

Pets are closer than family to many people, providing unconditional love and companionship in good times and bad. It has been noted that the loss of a pet can be harder to cope with than the loss of a family member.

Given the bonds of love that form between people and their animal companions, it comes as little surprise that reports of animal spirits make up a considerable percentage of the ghostly accounts submitted to FATE. Animal lovers take great comfort in the assurance that dogs, cats, and other creatures may also experience a life beyond the earthly plane.

Echoes of Melody

We had a little beagle named Melody, who wasn't a watchdog and served no other purpose than being a loving pet. We have a fenced yard, so our beagle stayed outside all day. Every night, just like clockwork, she scratched on the door to be let inside at precisely eight o'clock. We would open the door and she would scamper inside to spend the night.

Like all pets do, Melody got old. One morning, well into her mid-teens, we found her unable to get to her feet. We carried her to the vet, and there wasn't anything that could be done for her except to put her out of her misery. Reluctantly, we let the vet put her to sleep, and we petted her until she fell into her final sleep. That afternoon, we brought her home and buried her on the bluff, overlooking the river.

That night, we were sitting around the kitchen table, mourning her and talking about all the funny, loving, or stupid things she had done in her lifetime. We were interrupted by scratching on the door. Looking at the clock, we saw it was exactly eight o'clock. I ran to the door and opened it, but there was nothing there.

For about a week, every night at eight o'clock there was a scratching at the door. And every night, one of us opened the door, even though we knew there wasn't anything there. And we would hold the door wide open for a minute or so, even though we knew that there would be no Melody to scamper inside. Still, it was the least we could do.

—*Connie Kutac,*
Farmington, N. Mex.

Cinnamon

In 1976, my friend Mary Dalby lived in Tempe, Arizona, with her beautiful cat Cinnamon. Cinnamon looked like the cat on the Purina Cat Chow bag. He loved to walk with her, and always stayed close to her side. Cinnamon and I became friends. He always sat in my lap. He let me hold him close. His soft breath tickled my neck and his heavy purring told me he was happy.

One day Mary was mowing her lawn. Cinnamon became playful, ran close, and batted at the mower. The blade cut his foot. After several visits to the veterinarian, the paw was healed, but it was now about three times its normal size. The veterinarian said it would always be extra large. Cinnamon used his large paw to his advantage, making sure everyone noticed it.

My work kept me away for several weeks. One day, Mary called and asked me to have dinner with her. When I arrived Cinnamon was lying by the open door to the backyard. He came running to my side and started wrapping himself around my legs. His cries were so loud, I reached down and picked him up. He started hitting me with his large paw, as if to say, "It's me, Cinnamon." Then he laid his head against my neck. I put him down and he looked up at me, making eye contact. Our eyes locked and the most wonderful, spiritual feeling filled my being with so much love.

Once inside the house, I told Mary about my encounter with her cat. She got a strange look on her face and said, "That can't be true, my cat died three weeks ago."

I was dumfounded. Then I realized what a wonderful message that Cinnamon had given me. It was so real; when I lifted him up I felt his weight and his soft fur. I know now why he was hitting me with his large paw—he wanted me to know it was him.

Thank you Cinnamon for materializing for me. You gave me proof of survival.

—*Verial Swift,*
Scottsdale, Ariz.

Cat Apparitions

About 14 years ago a hungry stray cat showed up at our home. We had a small kitten, who enticed the larger cat to come into our house for dinner. The stray cat was scared and edgy, eating just a little and then skedaddling off. Later, our kitten was hit by a truck and killed, but the stray cat kept coming back. He built up some trust with us over a few weeks. I named him Claude.

We were getting ready to move across town and I was concerned about what would happen to him. I decided to try to move him with us. I kept Claude inside our new home for a day and then let him loose. He stayed for five years.

I really loved that cat. He would occasionally go out on a "tom trip" and be gone for a week or so. He always came back, so I felt no cause for alarm. Then one time he left and was gone for only a day, but I knew that he was dead. I voiced my fear to my husband, who tried to reassure me that he hadn't been gone long enough for me to worry. The next day, however, as I was vacuuming the rug, I saw Claude sitting there patiently, waiting for me to notice him. When I did, he looked me in the eye and communicated that he was sorry. Then he disappeared. He never did come back, so I knew he had come to say goodbye.

Several years later, I had another cat and named him Tom. Now, Tom really loved me. One evening, he did not come home. The next morning, he showed up outside the garage door. He was very sick and his back legs were paralyzed. He had dragged himself home. I immediately took him to the vet and left him. The vet did not know what was wrong. The next day, the vet said Tom was better and he just might make it. He thought that maybe Tom had eaten a poisonous lizard.

That night I was sitting at my kitchen table talking with a friend, and Tom appeared by my feet and looked up at me. He then went to the refrigerator, walked over to his bowl, and disappeared.

"Oh! Tom is dead," I said as I watched him walk across the room. My friend saw nothing.

The next morning I called the vet to check on Tom and was told that Tom had died during the night. Tom, too, had come to say goodbye.

—*Serenda Jenks,*
Fairdealing, Mo.

Polkie and Arnie

It's hard to lose your pets after having them for many years and to lose two of them was almost unbearable. Polkie was my dominant cat, Arnie his passive brother. I had them since they were born, October 24, 1986; nearly 20 years, almost half my life. Their mother was with us for 17 years before her body finally gave out. We always figured she'd lived so long because she didn't want to leave her kitties.

Polkie went first on May 16, 2006. While dozing, he suffered a stroke and woke up blind and bewildered. The only humane thing to do was to put him to sleep and set him free. Although I loved all my cats, Polkie and I had a special relationship. He was my baby, my confidant, my lap cat. He was my Polkaroos. Letting him go was one of the hardest things I've ever had to do.

I'm a true believer in the afterlife and fully expected to receive a visitation dream or some other type of evidence from Polkie that he was well and okay on the other side. Two days after he died, I felt a cold air mass pass over my arm and face while lying in bed. I knew it was Polkie waking me up, touching my nose with his, just like he had every morning for as long as I could remember. But still I didn't want to let him go and I begged for more signs to satisfy my grief.

The next morning I woke to him walking up my back, something he did to get me to get up and feed him. When I rolled over he was gone. I was grateful for his visits, but still wanted him to come in a dream so that I could see him one more time.

Arnie was also lonesome for Polkie, even though we had adopted another cat a couple years prior for the sole purpose that when one of the old boys went the other wouldn't be alone, neither of them ever having been without the other. We wanted to make the transition for the survivor as easy as possible.

Summer went on and with each passing day I knew it was getting closer to the time I would have to put Arnie down. It was hard enough losing one brother, but to lose them both meant that it was the end of an era and that the cycle of life had continued beyond my control.

October 23, 2006, the day before he would turn 20 years old, I came home to an ailing fluffy orange cat whom I'd loved since he was a wet kitten from his mother's womb. Knowing it was time to send him to be with his brother, I kissed him one last time and told him to come back to me in a dream and to bring his brother with him so that I knew they were together and okay. I held him as the vet injected her serum and cried as the light dimmed from his eyes.

It was easier to let Arnie go knowing he was with Polkie. They were inseparable throughout life and now in death. They were old cats that lived good lives and gave us many wonderful memories. They were there during the good times and the hard times, always offering their unconditional love.

On November 2, 2006, in the middle of the night, they came to me in a visitation dream, both beautiful, young again, and full of life in all their splendor. I was so happy to see them that I woke up. Still conscious of their presence, the feel of their fur at my fingertips, their voices resonantly sounding in my inner ear, I knew I was fortunate to have had them in my life for as long as I did, and that they would always be with me.

Lying in bed, comforted with the knowledge they were together in the afterlife, I drifted back to sleep only to be awoken a couple hours later with the news that my 93-year-old grandfather had passed in the middle of the night. It seems my faithful companions came to comfort me once again, proving to me there is life after death. And with that knowledge, I know Grandpa isn't alone on the other side and his kindly old spirit is watching over me too.

—*Julie T. Petersen,*
Circle Pines, Minn.

Miss P.

On Friday night, May 12, 2006, I went to sleep with my four dogs. Several hours passed and we all slept soundly. I awoke to my dog Marilyn barking. Marilyn, a Corgi-Jack Russell mix, tends to become easily agitated in the night, so this was not uncommon. I sat up to soothe her and what I saw directly in front of us shocked us both. It was my mom's white Persian cat, Miss P., who had been dead for seven years.

I pulled Marilyn close to me. Her fur rose as Miss P. strolled by with her typical nonchalant little walk.

Once Marilyn ceased barking, I went back to sleep. Oddly, none of the other three dogs stirred during all of this.

That Sunday I went to have dinner with my parents, Sue and Chuck Ostermeyer. I related what Marilyn and I had witnessed. My mom smiled and told me that she often saw Miss P. slinking by out of the corner of her eye.

One of our earliest sightings of Miss P. occurred right after the three of us returned home after taking her to the vet to be euthanized. She'd been diagnosed with tongue cancer and was quickly failing. We had to make the toughest but kindest choice and have her put to sleep. We were driving home from the vet's and I looked up into the sky and there was a cloud that looked exactly like Miss P. running. I quickly pointed it out to my parents and the three of us were quite moved. It was as if she was communicating that everything was going to be okay.

My mom and I have always been very sensitive to spirits around us. I think Marilyn may have this same trait, but even more finely honed.

—*Laura Ostermeyer,*
Tucson, Ariz.

One Last Goodbye

The bond between people and animals has been the subject of many stories, some true, some imagined. What happened to me was most definitely true. I have a witness. Unfortunately, she'll never be able to tell the tale. It falls to me to relate what really happened.

Jacob, my sweet old cat, had reached the age of 20. He suffered several strokes that left him totally deaf and gave his walk a little shimmy. He was a member of my little household seven years before my first child was born, so we shared a particular relationship. He knew from a look or a nod what I wanted him to do and he always did it. He would sometimes sneak from shadow to shadow around the kitchen table when I wasn't looking to snatch the last bit of food left in the dog's bowl. All I had to do was catch his eye and give him my best angry look and he would quickly give up the adventure and slink into the next room. I got to know what he was feeling just by looking into his eyes.

Those last few days of his life were the hardest for me. Jacob was so brave. He wouldn't give in to death even when his internal organs stopped functioning. I knew that many times animals that know their death is near will run away and find a dark, quiet place to die alone. When he wasn't lying in his usual place by the kitchen door I knew I would have to search him out. He wouldn't get very far in his frail condition. I found him in the neighbors' cellar, way at the bottom of the steps, half submerged in dirty water. I knew what I had to do.

On the seat of the car, Jacob lay wrapped in a towel, purring very quietly as I stroked him. Even in his deteriorating condition he tried to make me happy as we drove to the animal hospital. The vet took one look at Jacob and told me gently it was time to put him to sleep. I handed him over to the nurse and as I did his eyes met mine for the last time. Those big yellow eyes were pathetic as he looked to me for comfort I could not give. I wanted to hold him while they gave him the shot, but the vet advised against it.

Jacob was taken into another room and I made my way out to my car and collapsed in tears, clutching the steering wheel. I never before experienced so great a loss. He was closer to me than any living thing, and a void in my life opened like a giant chasm.

I could hear the distant rumble of thunder as I started my car. I arrived home before the rain began. And when it did start, it was like weeping. I felt like the whole world was crying for this courageous animal. Jacob liked to sit on the windowsill and try to catch the drops of rain running down the window pane. As I watched them now making zigzag patterns on the glass, my own tears joined the procession and the ache in my chest intensified.

The next morning after breakfast, I grabbed the dog's leash and took Cindi, my little sheltie, for a walk. The rain had cleared off and the sun was shining on a crisp new day. Everything was still dripping and that wonderful smell of rainwater and freshly mowed grass filled the air. The sidewalks were still wet, and we had to skirt some of the puddles as we walked along.

We walked down a shady back street near our house. Long stretches of back lawn rippled down to the road on both sides like the swells of a great green sea.

As I walked along it suddenly became icy cold. The wind blew at me like an open freezer door. Cindi shook her head several times and I tried to calm my goose bumps by wrapping my arms around myself. Then Cindi saw something. She became alert and her ears stood straight up, the way dogs' ears do when they see a squirrel or another dog. She began straining at the leash.

As I followed the direction of her gaze, the breath stopped short in my lungs. I think I held my breath for a time. There in front of us, coming out from under a small bush, was Jacob. I knew it was him by his labored walk with the little shimmy and his thin, gaunt body. Cindi strained forward on the leash while I stood there unable to move.

When the cat got to the middle of the road, he turned and looked right into my eyes. The moment I saw those golden eyes, I felt a wave of comfort run right through me. It was as if he were telling me that everything was all right. The ache in my chest melted away as I stood there. I think I looked away for just a second to collect myself, and when I turned back again, Jacob was gone. I looked around and noticed that our footprints made outlines on the wet blacktop where we had walked, but Jacob's did not.

Cindi and I moved quickly the few feet to where Jacob had emerged from under the bush on the right side of the road. There was a large expanse of lawn to the left in the direction he had appeared, but no sign of Jacob. Cindi sniffed the ground for a little while and looked around in confusion. The chill had dissipated and there was no sign of Jacob. I caught myself turning around several times as we walked away. I was filled with wonder and it made me smile.

Later I described this experience to several people and they looked at me like I had lost my mind. A grief-stricken hallucination, they said. I might have believed them if I was alone at the time. But there was another witness: Cindi. She saw what I saw but she'll never be able to tell what happened. I only wish she could.

The bond between humans and animals is a mysterious thing and fills me with awe. For all their arguments to the contrary, no one will ever be able to convince me that Cindi and I didn't see Jacob that June morning. I still believe that somehow he knew what I was feeling and came back to say one last goodbye.

—*Diane Kolb,*
Melrose Park, Pa.

Healing Visions of Fritz

The families waiting in the veterinarian's office couldn't help but turn and look as Fritz walked in. He was an exceptional dog in every way. His grandmother had graced the cover of *Dog Fancy*, and his bloodlines guaranteed success at speed and agility. A few audible gasps could be heard as Fritz walked past, his silvery-gray coat glistening and shining in the morning sun. After a cursory glance, Fritz paid them no mind. He focused his attention on the task at hand: walking across the room. Despite his good looks and winning conformation, Fritz was a very sick dog.

Two weeks earlier doctors diagnosed him with canine hemolytic anemia, a serious but normally treatable condition. Fritz's system was attacking itself, and he could not produce enough red blood cells to sustain life. Normally alert and active, Fritz could now only lie down and heave for air. Initially, he responded to the massive doses of steroids prescribed by the doctor, but now his athletic frame failed him. His tongue and gums faded to a pale pink. Even the act of standing required extreme effort, causing him to lose control of his bladder. On this morning in September, Fritz took his last walk—but he did so with surprising dignity. His carriage and his noble expression let those around him know that he was a Shetland Sheepdog of the first order.

He came to me from the Showdown Shelties kennel in the spring of 1998 at seven and a half weeks of age. Fritz spent his first few years in the country, running and making impossibly graceful catches with Frisbees and balls. A run-in with a truck slowed him down a bit, but, in his prime, Fritz could sustain 35 miles an hour and turn on a dime. And he was smart.

I took a week off of work when Fritz arrived, and, within a few days, he was housetrained. Over the years Fritz and I developed a quiet form of nonverbal communication. I hesitate to call it telepathic, but I have no doubt that we communicated through our minds and spirit. I could think Fritz to come, and he would. I also came to rely on Fritz to interpret his environment for me. It was only after his passing that I fully realized how much I relied on him to run interference between the humans and dogs in our household. Fritz would tell me if Mickey wanted cuddling or Boris petting. Of course, no words were exchanged, but the ideas or concepts entered my mind from somewhere outside myself. The death of Fritz completely ended this process, and I have struggled to open new channels of communication with his surviving brothers.

His death left me reeling. A huge hole, uniquely filled by him, would have to heal like any other wound —slowly and over time. Dr. Horton did her best to quarterback the euthanasia, and she calmed his head as it shook and slowly sank in death. His one blue eye still sparkled as I left the room. I cried for five hours after I came home. The grieving process continued with staccato pain over the next week, and then something happened to stop it: a dream.

Now, I've never been a big dreamer—that is, I never paid much attention to dreams or even remembered them. This one was different. Fritz emerged from darkness and transferred feelings of happiness and excitement. He anticipated something splendid about to happen. He turned, gave me a loving look, and ran into the darkness. I immediately awoke with an overwhelming sense of peace and contentment.

From that moment onward, I have not grieved for Fritz. Originally, I marveled at the healing power of the human mind. I accepted the dream as some mysterious coping mechanism, and I awkwardly tried to broach the subject with my wife in this manner. Then: another night, another dream. Could there be something more at work here?

I can't offer my healing visions of Fritz as proof of his survival, only as my personal experience. These dreams suddenly and totally ended my grief. From that night on, I could remember and discuss my love for him without trauma. Suddenly and totally: aren't these words we use to describe miracles?

Change is constant, and, when I see Fritz again, I'm not sure what he will have become, but I am assured of his love and friendship. Because of his parting gift, I no longer have to grieve.

—*Daniel J. Wood,*
Three Rivers, Mich.

Crow Spirit

I have had some odd experiences with crows, but none as strange as one in January 2007. My hometown of Terre Haute, Indiana, is the winter roosting site for over 50,000 crows. The crows pour into the city every evening to avoid the hunters during crow hunting season.

This particular winter, my next-door neighbor captured a wounded crow and put it in a cage on his back porch. He is an artist, and he wanted to draw the crow for a crow art exhibit.

The crow did poorly, and one morning I saw it lying on its back. I took it to a vet who thought it had been poisoned by lead shot. He gave me some powdered bird food and vitamins to try to keep it alive. I fed the crow the best I could, but I got the impression that it disliked humans. I have been around birds all my life, and never have I felt a bird's dislike for me. The crow also had a strong metallic odor.

At 5:00 one morning I heard a clunk, like something had hit the side of a cardboard box. When I got up, I found the crow dead in its box. I put the box with the dead crow in the garage and went off to work.

A few mornings later, I awoke to the sound of an animal walking quickly, claws clicking on the wooden floor, along one side of my bed and then the other. Then I heard an animal crying like it was in great distress. I leaped out of bed thinking something had happened to one of my cats, but they were sleeping in the next room. As I got back into bed, I smelled the metallic odor of the crow.

At 5:00 the next morning, I was awakened again by the cries of an animal in distress. The sound seemed to be coming from midair in the center of the room. My cats were nowhere nearby. It suddenly hit me: it was the crow whose dead body I had left in the garage. I immediately got dressed and went out to bury the crow. I placed a stone above its grave to prevent any other animal from digging it up.

I have not heard any more cries. I had never before considered that a wild animal would want its body respected and laid to rest properly. I am left with the thought that intelligent animals like the common crow have a soul or spirit that survives death.

—*Margaret Moga,*
Terre Haute, Ind.

My Brutus

Dogs truly are man's best friend. My Brutus was a white and brindle American Bull Terrier, who looked remarkably like the dog from *The Little Rascals*. He was the sweetest, most loving dog I have ever known, loving life so much that he always wagged his strong, goofy tail and greeted every person and animal he ever came across. I never heard of a dog that cared so much for people, especially children. He loved to play with and protect them, like he himself was a human child.

Brutus was my roommate when I moved from home, so it had always been just us. I took him with me everywhere. He was my buddy, and loved to go for rides in the car. I took him to the store and to visit friends and family. People would get very disappointed if he wasn't with me. Everyone fell in love with him. My father used to say, "When Brutus leaves us, he's going to have the most funeral attendants any dog in history has ever had."

Brutus was there for every life change I had, from college graduation to getting married. I had someone say to me once, if there was such a thing as an award for the best dog that ever lived, it would be given to him. It's like he wasn't a dog, but something greater. It sounds implausible, but believe me when I say Brutus was some type of an angel. Almost everyone experiences an emotional bond with an animal in their lifetime, like a familiar of sorts. It's our emotional connection with nature. Brutus taught me so many things about myself without even speaking. We were meant to be a part of each other's lives.

So when he died last year at the age of 11, it was devastating, for me especially, but also for my friends and family. He had heart cancer, and I had the difficult decision of putting him to sleep. Amazingly, he was a trooper until the end. He even went for a short hike before we took him to the vet. It was Halloween day when he passed, which makes what happened even more amazing.

That evening was very emotional for my husband and I. As a spiritual person, and someone who believes in the afterlife, I wanted a sign to show me that Brutus was okay. As his owner and caregiver, I wanted the reassurance that he was not lost or scared wherever he was. I needed to know that he was fine and waiting for the day we would meet again.

Four days after he passed, I was in the living room working on a scrapbook for Brutus, when I glanced over at the picture I had placed where his bed used to be in front of the pellet stove. That's when I almost dropped. Behind the framed picture on the floor, within the pellet stove glass, was the image of Brutus. I did a double-take and questioned whether I was just desperately looking for the sign that I so needed, but to my amazement it was him. His angled profile from the neck up was smiling back at me through the glass.

I was so elated that he listened to my pleas for reassurance, and somehow in his infinite doggy wisdom passed this sign on to me. Everyone who saw it was shocked and amazed. That was my Brutus; he always shocked and amazed us all.

So for all of you pet lovers who have had a good friend pass on, be assured that they are waiting for us on the other side and are still connected to us. I can hardly wait to see my sweet, loving boy again.

—*Linda Glazebrook,*
Worcester, Mass.

8

Ghost Encounters of Children and Encounters with Child Ghosts

It is often speculated that children experience the unseen in ways that adults have forgotten. As we get older and learn more about how the world is "supposed" to work, we filter out a larger spiritual world that was once open to us.

Indeed, a large number of compelling ghost reports feature younger witnesses. In many of these, the ghost encountered can be identified as an older relative whom the child witness never met or knew about. That a spirit would take an interest in his or her descendents long after death certainly makes sense.

On the flip side of children's ghost reports are accounts, often quite poignant, of child ghosts. Those who die very young seem prone to confusion over finding themselves in the spirit world, and may linger close to the earthly world for a longer period of time.

The Old Lady

There is a special time in the evening when it is neither daytime nor night. There is still some light in the sky and you can see objects around, though not as distinctly as in broad daylight. It was at that time of day that I first saw the lady.

I was six years old and had been put to bed in the upstairs room I shared with my older sister, Jean. Jean was gone for the summer working as a live-in babysitter. I was lying in my bed when I had the strange sensation that someone else was in the room with me. I looked over at my sister's bed and saw a strange lady sitting there watching me.

I was frightened and a chill passed through me. I slid down in my bed and pulled the covers over my head. I couldn't help trembling but lay as still as I could. What should I do? I was afraid to get out of bed and run past her. I couldn't find my voice to scream. Very cautiously I moved the blanket just enough so I could peek out. She was still there exactly as before. She had not moved or made a sound. She didn't seem evil or threatening, but I couldn't understand why she was there or what she wanted. I tried to lie still and keep an eye on her, but I must have fallen asleep in spite of my fears, and when I woke up in the morning she was gone.

At breakfast I wanted to tell my family, but I was afraid my parents and brother might laugh at me or say I was just making up stories or I had been dreaming. I wasn't too sure myself, so I kept still and soon forgot about it.

A few nights later, she came again. It was the same time of evening when it was almost dark. Again I had the feeling that someone was in my room. I looked over at Jean's bed and there was the lady. Both my grand-mothers were dead and I couldn't remember them, but I thought she looked like a grandmother might. She had white hair pulled back from her face and done up in a bun and she wore a long dark dress and a white apron. She sat on the bed with her arms crossed over her chest rocking gently back and forth as if she was in a rocking chair. Again I fell asleep, and when I awoke she was gone.

After several more visits that summer I began to feel quite comfortable with her. She never said any-thing, but seemed content to sit quietly with her arms crossed watching me. I couldn't bring myself to tell anyone about her.

Fall came and my sister returned. She went to bed at the same time I did in the evening, but as she was older she often wasn't sleepy, so she would read me stories, or we'd sing nonsense songs that she had learned at camp, and we'd giggle until our mother called up from the bottom of the stairs, "You girls better hush up now and go to sleep."

Many years later my father had a stroke and was taken to the hospital. My mother and I took turns sitting by his bedside. He died after a few days.

I was visiting my mother one day shortly after his death when she said, "Something rather strange happened to me while I was sitting with your father in the hospital. It was that time in the evening when it was neither daylight nor dark and I was tired. He was resting quietly and I hadn't turned on the lights. I looked across the bed and there was a woman standing there looking down at him. I recognized her immediately—it was his mother. I thought to myself, of course, she is concerned about him and it's wonderful that she is here. I got out of my chair to go and greet her, but I looked again and there was no one there. I felt so foolish. She's been dead for over 30 years."

"You said it wasn't very light in the room, Mother," I said. "How did you know who it was?"

"Oh, I knew right away," she replied. "She looked just like she always did with her long dark dress and white apron, her hair pulled back in a bun, and her arms folded across her chest the way she always did. I'd like to think she was coming to meet him."

—Anne Nicholas,
Roseburg, Oreg.

A Cold Touch

One of my earliest memories is of a ghostly experience involving my aunt and me. My mom and dad had just moved into a house that had been used as a parsonage near a little country church. They boxed off half of the long back porch and made it into a small bedroom for me. From the back window, you could see the little graveyard beside the church. On the night my aunt came to visit, there was one new grave, completely covered with fresh-cut flowers.

My aunt decided to sleep with me since we had no extra beds and my room was the coolest one in the house. Of course, she looked out the window and saw the flower-covered grave.

"Who was just buried?" she asked my mother.

"You didn't know her," my mother said. "She and her husband moved here after you went away. She died in childbirth. Her husband took the baby back to his family in Ohio right after the funeral."

With a cool breeze blowing through the open windows, my aunt and I fell asleep immediately. I don't know what woke us, but both of us were suddenly awake. Then, the coldest thing I have ever felt touched my shoulder. I began crying at full volume, and my aunt reached over to comfort me. The cold hand touched her arm, and she began to scream. Her screams made the thing let go. Mom and Dad ran into the room to see what was happening.

"Something was in this room," my aunt told them. "I've never felt anything so cold!"

"There's nothing here now," my mother said, trying to soothe us. But then we saw Dad bend down and pick something up.

"I wonder how this got in here," he said. He held up a fresh funeral flower for us to see.

We wondered if that poor dead mother had come looking for her baby. And I wonder what would have happened to me if my aunt had not been there.

—*Lonnie E. Brown,*
Middletown, Ky.

My Opa

I was ten years old in 1977, and that summer I flew to Germany alone to see my grandmother—my "Oma," Elsa Roth. She lived alone as all her children were grown, married, and had families of their own. I never knew my Opa, Johannes Roth. He was killed in World War II.

I slept with my Oma in her bed—she on the right and I on the left. One night I settled into bed and had just fallen asleep when I was awakened by a very bright light. It seemed to come through the window. I assumed it was just a car with very bright headlights. I tried to go back to sleep, but the light was so bright.

Finally, I sat up and looked at the light. It wasn't so bright now, and a figure started to take form. He wore a drab green military uniform. I just stared at him as he walked to my side of the bed. He was very real—you couldn't see through him.

He leaned over, touched my hand (his hands were warm), and said, "So you are my American grand-daughter. I've always said I would come see you."

He had such a nice smile. Then he straightened, turned, and walked back to the window. There was no light—just stairs. He slowly climbed them until he disappeared.

I sat for a while trying to figure out what had happened. He spoke to me in English even though I know German. I never said a word to my Oma about it.

At home once again, months later, I mustered up enough courage to ask my mom, Gisela Tubiolo, if she believed in ghosts. She said she did and so I asked her why. This is what she told me:

"When I was a little girl, seven years old, my dad went away to war. I slept with my mom in her bed—I was on the left and she on the right.

"One night my dad appeared next to my side of the bed wearing his military uniform. He sat down and told me everything was okay, and that one day he would see his American granddaughter. He told me to be good for Mom and asked where she was. I told him she was in the living room. He got up, walked to the door, opened it, went through, and closed the door. I never saw him again.

"One week later there was a knock at the door and a military man brought Mom a telegram. It said that Dad was killed the week before. It was the same day and time when he came to visit us for the last time."

In the summer of 1990 I was 23 and went back to Germany with my 18-month-old son to visit my Oma. She had wanted to see her first great-grandchild since he was born.

We were looking at old photos one afternoon, and I asked her about how Opa died and how she found out about it. She said she knew he was dead before she was officially informed about his death. I asked her how she knew and she told me:

"One night, when the kids were sleeping, Opa came from the bedroom into the living room and sat next to me on the couch. He held my hands and told me what had happened. He said he was shot and that before he could leave this earth he had to come home and tell his family so they wouldn't worry.

"We talked about what would happen to all of us. He said all would be okay, and that one day he would come back to see his American granddaughter.

"He stayed for an hour and then had to leave. He walked to the living room door, opened it, and walked out. I never saw him again. One week later I got the news he was dead, but I already knew. There was no body to bury, as he fell near Russia."

In 1992 my Oma passed away. I know Oma and Opa are together now.

—*Marianne Bean,*
Security, Colo.

The Other Side

I must have been about six years old when I had my first experience with the other side. Like an antenna, I still tune in to spirits.

My parents had taken me to my grandparents' house for the summer. I always loved going there, so I was naturally thrilled.

As we pulled up, I could see a woman dressed in 18th-century clothing standing on the porch, watching us as we arrived. She was so pretty, with her long black hair draped over her shoulders.

"Mommy," I asked, "do you see the lady on the porch?"

My mother looked at me in such a strange way and said, "There is no one on the porch, Gloria. Quit playing around!"

As we walked up the pathway that led to the porch, I smiled at the lady. She nodded her head in a dignified sort of way, then faded into nothing before my eyes.

Somehow I knew right then and there that she was a spirit. Later that evening Grandma tucked me into bed, gave me a kiss, and shut out the light.

I fell asleep shortly thereafter. Much later, I was awakened by a feeling of somebody crawling into bed with me. When I looked to see who it was, there was no one there.

It's kind of funny, but I was not scared. I just drifted back to sleep without hesitation.

The next morning, I jumped out of bed to use the bathroom, and who did I see but the same lady from the day before standing by my bed and smiling.

"Gloria, time for breakfast!" called Grandma from downstairs.

"Just a minute," I yelled back. I finished washing my hands and came out of the bathroom. The lady had disappeared once again.

I hurried down the stairs for breakfast. Ham and eggs are my favorite, and Grandma knew that. She even made me toast with strawberry jam.

While eating, I told Grandma about the spirit lady. She took out an old photo album and sat down beside me. We went through it together.

About halfway through, I saw a picture of the pretty lady I'd seen. Grandma looked at me with such amazement and said, "That's my mother's great-grand-mother, who died in this house."

—Gloria Lee Lewis,
Portland, Oreg.

A Dose of Chicken Soup

I was born in 1972, years after my great-grandmother had passed away. Nevertheless this woman will always hold a place in my heart. Even though it is true that I never met her in the flesh, at least I have had the opportunity to meet her as a spirit.

It was late one night in about 1985 or '86 while I was staying in my great-grandmother's home with my grandmother. Feeling very sick with a sore throat, I had stayed in the house by myself while my grandparents had gone out to dinner with friends. I tried to keep myself occupied as I lay on the couch watching televi-sion. But I could not shake the thought that someone else was there with me.

At 11:00 p.m., this feeling grew stronger as the television seemed to turn off by itself. It was very puz-zling to see the knob turn without anyone actually touching it. I could not believe my eyes when a few minutes later the radio seemed to come on. Things were beginning to get really interesting. From out of nowhere I heard the soft voice of an elderly woman.

"Do any of you kids want to listen to Amos and Andy with me?"

Knowing I was the only one in the house, I proceeded to look around. As I neared the kitchen, I could see the small glowing figure of a woman standing by the sink. I instantly knew that this woman was not my grandmother. As I stood there in awe, the woman walked right through me into the living room. Really starting to feel scared, I ran back to the couch and hid under the blanket.

"What is wrong with you?" she asked, calling me by my father's name.

I told her that my throat hurt, and she offered me a cup of chicken soup. I refused, but she insisted that she was there to check on her house and relatives within it. After 20 minutes or so, I agreed to try some of the soup. She told me that she would be back in a second or two, and then vanished.

Upon her return, she carried a small cast iron pot and a tin cup. As I looked into the containers, I could not see anything, but the smell of warm chicken broth filtered through my nostrils. The very instant she held the cup to my lips, the soreness in my throat seemed to disappear. I tried to thank her, but she just waved goodbye and told me that she had to go.

It was amazing to see the way she moved. Her feet seemed to glide about three inches off the floor as if she just floated from one place to another. Still trying to get her name, I followed her as fast as I could, and as far as I could. But she walked right through the bathroom wall, and I knew that I would never get an answer from her.

A few months later, I was finally told who this person was. My mother and I were helping my aunt set up for a yard sale when I decided to tell them what I had seen in my grandparents' house. As I described how the woman looked and what she wore, my aunt sat in amazement looking at me. She told me that the woman I saw and talked to was her long-dead grandmother, and she began to tell me a little about her.

Feeling that this woman was very special, and knowing how she came back to help me, I knew I had to remember her in my own way. So when my daughter was born, my wife and I tried to think of a nice name for her. We finally tried calling her by my great-grandmother's name. When our baby looked and seemed to smile at us, we knew that it had to be her name.

—*Christopher L. Booth,*
Nampa, Idaho

Aunt Bertha

Not every old house is haunted, but the three-story brick Victorian home where I grew up had its share of paranormal activity. Most of it was minor; small things like faint voices, footsteps, and strange sounds. On occasion, a small appliance might turn on without assistance or lights might come on in the early morning hours without being touched.

We were accustomed to the quirks of the house, and the unexplained happenings failed to frighten us. Although we sensed more than one presence (one male, one female) in the house, we gave a name to just one, the feminine spirit that we dubbed "Aunt Bertha" in honor of one of the home's former residents. The real Bertha was alive and well but the name seemed to suit.

Three events stand out as the most spectacular demonstrations of supernatural activity, and each happened to me.

One summer night I awakened to find what I thought was my mother standing beside my bed. As I opened my mouth to ask her a question, I realized that the features of the woman were strange to me and that the gown she wore was old-fashioned, nothing like my mom's polyester nightgown. Paralyzed with fear, I shut my eyes and lay still as she pulled the sheet over me and tucked me in.

On another occasion, we were at my aunt's home across town when she and my mother played a joke on me that was not quite funny. Using the upstairs phone extension, my aunt pretended to be "Aunt Bertha," but I recognized her voice. Undaunted, I dialed my home number and was stunned when a sweet female voice answered.

"Is this Aunt Bertha?" I stammered.

"Why, yes, that's what you call me."

Fear and excitement warred inside me as I asked, "Do you always answer the phone?"

"Only when no one is here."

When I asked if she was always in the house, she laughed. "Yes, I am; I'm here just floating around."

During the strange conversation, my mother and aunt urged me to quit playing around. To this day, neither they nor I understand just who (or what) I talked to that day.

The third encounter was by far the most dramatic. After our family moved to another city, we put the house up for sale and took my cousins on a last-chance tour of the empty home. My cousins, all boys, disputed the idea that the house could be haunted. Now a bold 16-year-old young lady, I told them that I would prove it.

We had gathered in the large living room where a glass chandelier with six circles of individual prisms hung from the ceiling. I called out to whatever entities might be present and told them that some among us did not believe. "Show us a sign," I said.

The atmosphere around us shifted from the stale air of an unoccupied house to a heady, expectant sense, something like the dead calm before a storm. We waited and a single prism on the chandelier began to sway. I think everyone present held their breath as my mother softly whispered, "Look!"

One by one the prisms on one circle danced as if touched by an unseen hand until that particular circle was in motion.

In one collective motion, we all turned to look at the closed storm windows and the storm door, also shut. There was not a breath of air moving through the house and even had there been a breeze, it would have been unlikely if not impossible that wind could move the prisms in such a precise fashion.

There were no more unbelievers as we departed my old home for the last time. To this day, we still tell stories about our haunted house. Strangest of all is the talk around the old neighborhood that odd things continue to happen there on a regular basis.

—*Lee Ann Sontheimer Murphy,*
Neosho, Mo.

A Series of Paranormal Events

In my lifetime I have encountered many strange occurrences that have at times made others doubt my sanity and even have thoughts of sending me to a facility for psychological care. For the first encounter, we must travel back several years to my days in elementary school.

My family moved into a new home, and for the first time I had my very own room. Like any other little girl, I decorated with ponies, books, dolls, and even a doll house. In the winter I had to sleep in the guest room on the other side of the house because it was warmer, so my room became my playroom for the cold months.

Several times in the evening when I would go to my playroom, I saw her. Standing before my dollhouse looking sad and alone was a girl around my age. For the longest time, she would immediately disappear when she saw me. At first my parents believed I was just a child with a very overactive imagination.

After a few months, the girl began staying longer and longer, but it would be still longer before the first words were spoken. Maybe it took that long for me to be ready to hear her. Soon we became friends, and to my dismay that was the one thing keeping her from crossing over. She had died so young that she had never really had a friend. By this time my parents began scheduling sessions for me to meet with the school guidance counselor.

My next encounter was at the age of 12. My family lived out in the country and my parents worked an hour from our home, so I spent most of my time with a babysitter. Four months after I started staying there, I began to hear odd noises: a bell that sounded similar to one on a cat's collar, but there was no cat, no animal of any kind. And a clock that had no batteries and was not plugged in that would chime.

The lady I was staying with began to suspect that I could also hear these sounds, so she sat down with me one day. In her hands was a photo album. She showed me pictures of a pretty girl who wore a decorative bell in every picture. One photo was taken at Christmas when she gave my sitter (who, it turns out, was the girl's mother) the clock.

As she flipped to the final page in the book, my sitter stared at my face for reaction to what I was seeing. On this page there was an obituary and pictures of a horrific car accident that had claimed the life of her daughter. Soon my parents would take me out of her care, stating it was an unhealthy environment for me to be in.

From a very young age my life has been changed by events which no one ever believed happened; well, no one but the sitter I was taken from. She understood because she was like me. Once and for all, I am ready to let others like me know they aren't alone

—Linda Williams,
Martinsville, Ind.

The Little Ghost Boy

We had just moved into an old two-story home in the historic district of Morgan City. I was alone in the house with my two-year-old son Matthew one night during our first week there when I was startled awake by a child's loud sobbing. I immediately jumped out of bed and ran downstairs, thinking that Matthew had wandered from his bedroom and forgotten where he was. I searched the entire downstairs looking for him. When I got to the laundry room the crying stopped.

I ran back upstairs and opened my son's door. There he was, sleeping soundly in his bed. I didn't know what to think. I knew I had heard a child crying, and I knew I hadn't been dreaming because it had continued during my search. Baffled, I went back to bed.

Several months later I found out I was expecting another baby. One afternoon as I was sitting on the sofa at the bottom of the stairs, I looked up and saw a little boy walking from one end of the hall to the other. He looked to be about two years old with blond hair, and he was wearing a red shirt and blue shorts. I would have assumed it was Matthew, except I could see through him. He quickly faded away.

I didn't tell anyone about the sighting. It didn't take long for me to talk myself out of believing I had seen the ghost. My mind kept coming up with rational explanations. The only problem was that I knew better.

I saw him again two weeks later. The little boy walked slowly across the hall, and he stared at me with a serious look on his face. It began to happen so often I could no longer explain it away. Eventually, the fear left me and I was filled with curiosity. I wanted to know who he was, and why he had chosen to show himself to me.

I asked a former occupant of the house if she had ever seen anything strange there, and she said that she had not.

When I told my husband about the little boy, he said I had too much time on my hands and needed a hobby. I was furious. Then, one night when our son was spending the night at his grandmother's house, we got home from a Lamaze class together and my husband headed upstairs. He quickly ran back down and showed me the goose bumps on his arms.

"I saw your little ghost," he said.

He wanted to leave the house and never return. I reminded him that the boy was harmless and we went to bed.

One night shortly after giving birth, I was sitting up in bed trying to soothe my new daughter. She suffered from colic and was inconsolable. I noticed the rocking chair across the room was rocking by itself. I had a shirt hanging from the back of it, so there is no mistake that it was moving on its own. I knew it was the little ghost boy. This was the last time he made his presence known. I don't know if the new baby frightened him away, or if it was the constant crying. We moved three months later.

—Paula Kennerson,
Lockridge, Iowa

Break Something

When I was 11 years old, my mother decided to tell me the truth about her sickness (she had metastatic liposarcoma). I had already known that the cancer was bad, but what she told me was that it was her death.

Imagine the shock of those words, and that she needed me to be strong. I remember sitting in her hospital bed, and crying into an old pillow. Finally, the tears all gone, I looked my mother straight in the face and said:

"Mom, I need you to promise me that when you die, you will break something that cannot be broken. It has to happen within a week or two of your death. If nothing breaks, then that means you went to Hell."

Needless to say, my mother promised to do what she could to prove that Heaven existed.

Two weeks after this speech on January 21, 1991, my mother died in a hospice. I stayed home the next day from school. I was in a daze, and decided to make myself a cup of Nestlé Quik. I removed a purple shatter-resistant mug from the cupboard, placed it on the middle of the table, and turned around to open the refrigerator. As I went to pour the milk into the mug, I saw the mug do a flip off the center of the table. It then hit the floor and shattered.

I looked at the mess on the floor, and then looked out the kitchen window with a happy smile. My mother had sent an immediate response.

I told this story to my three siblings, and two agreed that is was indeed an angelic message from our mother. All I knew at the time was that I was able to go back to school, deal with teen angst, and not be afraid of dying.

From time to time, sometimes I feel that my mother is still watching over her brood. A certain smell of Anais Anais or cilantro will have me looking over my shoulder. My mother and I were very close even though we did not have a long time to get know each other. She is always in my thoughts, and I hope to see her again.

—Renata Ramirez,
Daly City, Calif.

Two Little Girl Ghosts

I lived in a haunted house for ten years in the small Marin County town of Belvedere, California. It was a three-story, brown shingle house situated on a hill overlooking San Francisco Bay. Built in 1896 and remodeled several times, there was at least one family that never left—as I was to discover after my husband died in 1978. That is when things began to happen—footsteps, knocks, voices, apparitions, cooking smells, gray shadowy figures in my bedroom, and other incredible events.

One day in mid-August, 1978, I was napping on the sofa in the sunroom, which had been an outdoor porch and was now enclosed by windows. Above my sofa was the original window looking into the living room, sealed shut by many coats of paint. I was half-awakened by the now-familiar sounds of voices and scampering feet. I lay quietly, hoping I might see "them."

In that hazy state of mind I noticed the sealed-shut window above me was open, and two little girls—about eight or nine years old—were standing on the other side, leaning over the windowsill and peering at me in the wiggling manner that little girls are prone to. The child closest to me had long, light brown hair, and the other little girl had dark, curly hair—I couldn't see how long it was.

Even though I was in some kind of altered state of awareness, I was alert and knew that for the first time I was actually seeing the ghosts in my house. This was my chance to prove that they existed. Struggling to speak and form words they could understand, I managed to whisper, "Who are you?"

The brown-haired girl answered with something that could have been "Alice March," or "Alice LaMarch," or "Alice Marsh"—she didn't pronounce the name distinctly. The dark-haired girl gave her first and last name, but I could hear only the surname, "Knox"—this was very clear.

I repeated these names several times so I would remember them when I came out of that mental state. As the apparitions faded, I was still repeating "Knox, Marsh." I got up, went to my desk, and wrote an account of what happened, with every intention of investigating those two names at a later date.

Several weeks after the appearance of the two little girls, the name "Knox" came up in a conversation some friends of mine were having about local history.

Years later, in August 1984, I found the names "Knox" and "Marsh" while reading a book entitled *Old Marin With Love*. The book indicated that these families were among the early settlers of Marin County.

In 1997, I was reminiscing with my grandson Cary about the "spooky" Belvedere house (as he described it), when he suddenly exclaimed: "Once I saw a little girl ghost there!"

He couldn't remember the year, but he was a teenager at the time. He was sitting on that same sofa in the sunroom when he heard giggling. Turning around and looking through the window into the living room, he saw a little girl with long light-brown hair, running across the room. Then she disappeared.

All in all, none of the eerie events occurring in that house were harmful—they aroused more curiosity than fear.

—*Arlene Colvan,*
Astoria, Oreg.

9

Phantom Vehicles and Buildings

Ghost trains, phantom ships, and vanishing mansions are great topics for old-time folk ballads or spooky fiction, but not the sort of thing that one comes across in the real world, right?

On the contrary. As reported in FATE, all manner of phantasmal conveyances roll over lonely highways, ghostly Spanish galleons drift silently through the foggy Atlantic, and that strange house you saw in the woods may never reappear.

As with apparitions of living beings, some of these inanimate phantoms appear to be psychic recordings of some sort, insubstantial images burned into the environment for reasons unknown. In other cases, witnesses report taking rides in unearthly automobiles or entering buildings that can never be located again. These are among FATE's most perplexing stories.

Hear That Lonesome Whistle

On a brisk October morning in 1993, Rosemary and Mike Post fed their horses. Nothing seemed unusual. It was about nine o'clock, and the daily routine of caring for the animals was well underway. The barn is near the house. An abandoned railroad track borders the back of the property on State Route 665, about five miles from London, Ohio. Familiar sounds of buckets banging, water running, tack being hung, straw being shaken, and an old horse snorting "Good Morning" welcomed the day.

Then, a distant whistle disrupted the rural scene. Both Rosemary and Mike looked up from their work and tilted an ear in the direction of the noise. They glanced at each other in astonishment. Both stopped chores and headed toward the track. The sound was definitely a train whistle. Two long and two short horn blasts seemed to grow resoundingly louder.

The Posts expected to see something to explain the whistle—maybe some sort of railroad vehicle coming by. Nothing! They saw nothing coming down the track, or road, or anywhere. Yet the unmistakable blasts of a train whistle overpowered the busy clamor of the barnyard.

Rosemary was intrigued by morning's strange episode. She told her neighbors about the whistle without the locomotive. Two old farmers recalled a horrible railroad accident that occurred near the Upper Glade Run Cemetery. To the best of their memory, it happened in October, around 1912. The cemetery is about one mile up the track from the Post's farm.

Armed with this tidbit of information, Rosemary wrote to a journalist to see if he could help solve the mystery. An article appeared in the *Columbus Dispatch*. It told of an inquiry made to the Interstate Commerce Commission Accident Bulletin for the years 1911 to 1913. No train wreck near London was confirmed during that time period.

After the article was published, others living nearby wrote to Rosemary affirming that they, too, had heard a distinctive train whistle on that October morn.

The granddaughter of the doomed train's engineer contacted the Posts. She was shaken by the story. She told them her granddad died in the accident. According to her information, the train crashed and then exploded. Her grandfather and a fireman were scalded to death in the steam engine's explosion. Another man, a conductor, lived but was badly injured. She was uncertain of the year.

I heard this tale from my friend Jean, whose grand-father was an engineer. When he passed on, his engineer's log was handed down to the next generation. Browsing through the yellowed pages, his son noticed a special entry made in October 1930. The sorrowful entry described a train accident. Though not involved, he was truly moved by the tragedy. According to his account, the locomotive's steam engine had erupted. Both the engineer and fireman were decapitated in the explosion. The disaster happened near Glade Run Road between London and West Jefferson.

We wanted to know more about the train wreck and the ghostly whistle. First, we tried to locate Upper Glade Run Cemetery. On our second try, we spotted the overgrown headstones. A railroad crossing could be seen in the distance.

Jean and I climbed out of the car and walked along the track. The rails were sparkling in the setting October sky. We stopped cold and rigid. It couldn't be! It wasn't possible. We glanced at each other. I knew immediately she had heard it, too. A distant whistle broke the silence of the harvested fields.

"Did you hear that?" I asked.

"Yeah! Guess this isn't an abandoned track," she surmised.

Again the whistle sounded from afar. Cautiously and a little fearfully, we looked down the track. A round light was moving toward us. Soon the shape of a train was obvious through the dusky haze.

Jean stayed a safe distance nearby. I wanted a picture, so I ran to a small mound of gravel several feet from the track. The ground quaked. The earth shook and a whistle ripped through the air so loud my ears screamed with pain.

We watched the train disappear in a cloud of dust. It looked shadowy, unreal. When nothing more could be seen, the quiet was hollow. We felt eerie, so we left.

Are souls lost in a time warp still blowing the train whistle hoping to avoid a tragedy? Jean and I wonder. Did we really hear a whistle? Did we really see a raging train? We intend to investigate the area further. But we are not anxious to hear that terrifying whistle ever again.

—*Susan Carol Parker,*
London, Ohio

Angel on a Dark Road

Twenty years after the incident, that cold night remains in my mind—the night an unknown stranger saved my daughter and me from freezing to death on a lonely country road.

Her fiancé had cancer and it was spreading uncontrollably. He had returned to spend his last days with his parents and had asked her to join him as soon as possible. I was not surprised when her phone call came. "Mom, I need you." Two women and a large dog in a small car in the middle of winter set out on a mission, not knowing what to expect at our destination.

The long road trip across 11 states had brought us within a few miles of our goal. Darkness fell and snow began falling. Ice began to form on the car windshield, and visibility clouded from inside as the large dog, no doubt sensing our uneasiness, panted and drooled in the back seat. The supply of washer fluid quickly depleted as we struggled to stay free of dirty slush thrown up by passing cars.

Suddenly, the road grew deserted and we found ourselves alone on a highway that seemed to have no end. Tollways on the East Coast have many confusing twists and exits that seem to lead only to more exits. A look at the gas gauge showed we were running dangerously low on fuel. Terrified, we looked in vain for some sign of civilization, some lights to show there might be help in finding our way. All we saw were automated tollbooths, as if the world was being run by robots and we were the only people on a deserted road leading to nowhere. Where was everybody?

I thought of other times I had needed help finding my way and once again I prayed that God would send someone or something to guide us out of the maze we felt trapped in. Nothing happened for what seemed a long time. The wipers kept smearing slush over the windshield. The gas gauge indicator kept dropping toward empty. At each tollbooth devoid of human beings, I jumped out to wipe the headlights with my scarf. We would have to spend the night in this car. How would we survive the cold? The dog began to whimper and I knew that all three of us were hungry.

Suddenly a light shone by the side of the road. A small café appeared and we quickly pulled up in front. Hurrying through the door, I noticed that there was only one person inside. He seemed ready to close up. Putting aside my fatigue and confusion, I explained how we had been going in circles off one toll road and onto another. I told him as calmly as I could the address of the place we had been looking for. The man's serene manner put me at ease as he spoke softly. Yes, he said, the area we were looking for was two exits back, not hard to find if one knows what sign to look for.

I am not proficient in following directions, but expert at getting lost. Somehow, though, I grasped what he was saying and a sense of peace settled on me. Back in the car, I relayed the instructions to my daughter. Within five minutes we were in a warm house, sipping hot tea, thankful to be safe with our mission accomplished.

The next day, fortified by a night's rest, a full gas tank, and a fresh supply of washer fluid, we retraced our steps of the night before. We drove that stretch of road several times, looking in vain for a café that was not there.

—Ann Brandt,
Broomfield, Colo.

The Black Stagecoach

The night was a cold, brisk one, typical for November in the Arizona desert. It was about midnight when my belief system took a 180-degree turn.

We were returning from Thanksgiving dinner with family in Scottsdale. The road back to our home in Apache Junction was called McKellips Road. There was no one else on the road. The only light besides our headlights was that of the stars and the moon, which can be very bright in the Arizona night sky.

As I was driving along heading east, I noticed some extremely bright lights coming up on the driver's side at a very fast speed. I was traveling about 60 miles an hour, and this vehicle was approaching very quickly. As it came closer, I noticed the light was more of a phosphorescent color than normal white vehicle lights.

Then it happened. The approaching vehicle came up alongside the car and proceeded to pass us. It was completely shrouded in a very intense phosphorescent light, and there seemed to be a fog surrounding it as well. The vehicle appeared to be a black stagecoach—it looked like an old hearse from the 1880s or 1890s. I could not see any horses or driver, but I did see two lanterns on the back that seemed to sway back and forth as the vehicle pulled in front of the car.

The fog, as well as the light, completely enveloped the area of my car even after this thing pulled in front of us. The surrounding air seemed to become a few degrees colder as this phenomenon passed us and pulled in front of the car.

A few seconds passed, and then it proceeded to veer to the right, off the road and into the desert. About 50 or 60 feet into the desert, the thing started to disintegrate with tiny explosions of light. Finally the fog disappeared, the lights faded, and the stage was gone.

I thought that I might be hallucinating, but I wasn't really that tired and I knew I was in an alert state of mind. I didn't say anything to my traveling companion, who had been looking out the windshield of the car. I knew if this thing were really there then she had to have seen it as well. No more than a few seconds passed before she blurted out in a somewhat frenetic tone of voice, "What the hell was that?"

I knew then I was not hallucinating or dreaming, and that we had both seen this phenomenon. We concurred that we had both seen what appeared to be a "Black Stagecoach."

After researching this area, we discovered that the exact geographical area was known as "The Valley of the Lost Souls." In the late 1800s, this route was a stage line that was frequently besieged by bandits who held up the stagecoaches. Not only robberies, but also killings of the stage drivers occurred.

I wonder why were we allowed to see into that dimension. More importantly, I know now that another dimension truly does exist, proof positive that there is a realm beyond death—the ultimate mystery.

—*Tom M. Marcellino,*
Apache Junction, Ariz.

Phantoms of the Sea

When he came on deck that morning, the first thing the sailor noticed was the calmness of the sea. In the dawn's twilight, the Atlantic was gray and nearly glass-smooth. Strange, he thought, especially when the night before the ship had rolled noticeably in the rough sea.

He yawned, hunched his shoulders against the cold air, and headed for the bridge at a leisurely pace. From the corner of his eye something caught his attention. It was another vessel, a destroyer. It looked like something right out of World War II. Fascinated, he watched the old ship as it moved in the same direction as his ship, yet drawing closer.

Even this inexperienced sailor realized that there was something eerie about the ship. "It didn't look right," he said. "There was no sign of life. No one was on deck. The bridge looked deserted." When the ancient destroyer came within about 100 yards of his ship, something even stranger happened. It became transparent. "Honest to God. You could see right through that thing," said the sailor. "And then, I swear, it just disappeared."

He ran to the bridge, and as soon as he got there he shouted, "Did any of you see that?" No one said a word, yet he knew he wasn't the only witness to the ghostly destroyer. "The expressions on those guys' faces told me I hadn't imagined it."

When my cousin, Chet, told me about his experience in 1968, shortly after his ship docked in New York harbor, I laughed and asked if they'd all been drinking from the same bottle the night before. What other explanation was there for all of them having had the same hallucination? Chet didn't think that was funny.

Since then I've met a number of men who spent years on the oceans of the world aboard freighters, tankers, military ships, and even passenger vessels. Some were deck hands, others were officers. Regardless of rank, when I've told them about Chet's "hallucination," none have been surprised. They all say more or less the same thing: Chet saw a ghost ship.

At the same time, few have admitted to seeing ghost ships themselves. Most have been reluctant to describe encounters with these phantoms of the sea, fearing ridicule or that their sanity will be questioned. Nonetheless, as one listens to their stories, it's hard not to believe them.

"The first time I saw a ghost, I was scared to death," admits Padriac O'Kelly. O'Kelly first went to sea at the age of 16, and for over 45 years shipped out on everything from sailing vessels to modern tankers. There is no doubt in his mind that ghost ships roam the world's oceans.

"The first ones I saw were a fleet of Spanish galleons, believe it or not," he says in his still-thick Irish brogue. "It was in about 1928 or '29. I'd only been shippin' out for a year or so, but I remember it well."

His ship was in the middle of the Atlantic sailing from England to New York. "I was on the mornin' watch. There was patches of fog all around us, when from one of those fog banks out sails three galleons directly in front of us.

"Their sails were full as if they were bein' driven by a stiff wind, and they were heeled over and really goin'. But it was dead calm around us."

O'Kelly denies they were an optical illusion or the result of a tired mind playing tricks. "They were as plain as could be, not more than a couple of hundred feet away, and you could see everything, every detail."

On the main sail of each sailing ship was a huge red cross, and standards were flying from each ship. There wasn't, however, a single person to be seen on board the strange crafts, and they were totally silent. "If they'd been real ships, you could have heard the sails snappin' and the ships strainin'," says O'Kelly. "There was nothin' but quiet, though."

One thing that convinces O'Kelly that the ships weren't just in his mind is the fact that the images lasted so long. He remembers closing his eyes, shaking his head as if to make the ships go away. It didn't work. The three galleons plowed on through the water and vanished into another fog bank. "I'd never seen anythin' like it," says O'Kelly. But it wasn't his last encounter with ships that weren't there—at least not physically.

Off the coast of Africa in 1948, O'Kelly was aboard a ship bound for Australia when he saw an old Greek tanker he'd once served on. "I'd have recognized her anywhere," he said with a broad smile. "She was old, real old, and rode bad in the water, always rollin' and pitchin'.

"I'd heard she'd gone down, but when I saw her I thought, 'well, by God she didn't sink after all.'" Then he realized the slow-moving ship was totally silent. "That ship had an engine you could hear for miles, clankin' and a-clunkin' away. But she was stone quiet this time."

He soon learned it was silent for good reason. As the ship came closer, the tanker just faded away. Was O'Kelly frightened? "You're damned right I was scared. Not just because it was a ship I'd served on, but because I could see people on it. There was sailors all over the deck movin' around as if workin'."

According to O'Kelly, and other sailors who admit seeing ghost ships, they can appear just about anywhere. While they can show up anytime, they are most commonly spotted in the early morning or early evening when the sea is calm and the sun is below the horizon, yet the sky is still lighted by its rays. All types of vessels have been spotted, from Viking sailing craft to modern ships. The only apparent common denominator is that the ghosts are ships that sank.

Jay Green was in the merchant marine for nearly 30 years. He sailed the world, but spent most of his time in the Pacific. Now 75 years old, he recalls the only ghost ship he ever saw. It was in 1949. "We'd left Honolulu headed for San Francisco. Nothing unusual happened until we'd been out about two days."

Another sailor and Jay were sitting in the fantail of the ship when a huge square-rigged sailing ship came into view. "It didn't surprise me when my buddy says, 'Would you look at that.' Why shouldn't he say something; it isn't every day you see a square-rigger. Besides, it looked real enough."

The old ship moved slowly through the water, its sails barely flapping. Crewmen could be seen scurrying about the deck. The ship captivated Green and his partner, when another sailor walked by and asked them what they were looking at so intently. "We turned to look at him, and said 'that square-rigger,' or something like that. And he said, 'what square-rigger?' When we turned around it was gone." It was as if the third sailor had intruded on the private visitation of the ghost ship.

"Later, when we were alone, I asked my buddy to describe what he saw," recalled Green. "His description matched what I'd seen perfectly. I'm certain we were seeing the same thing—whatever it was."

Apparently it isn't uncommon for more than one person to see the same ghost ship at the same time, which is one reason why it is so difficult to write them off as simply the imagination of sea-weary sailors. Sometimes their sightings are recorded in the ship's log; more often they go unreported.

It is common practice for officers on one ship to log sightings of other ships by time of day and position. In the event a ship gets into trouble, this information is invaluable in helping plot the troubled ship's true course and approximately where it might be found. Ghost ships generally don't receive recognition. After all, they don't truly exist any longer.

Sailors are generally a superstitious lot. Most believe that the sighting of a ghost ship is an omen that their ship is destined for trouble. Many rationalize that, if they don't admit seeing them, then the sighting never took place and their ship is secure.

When sailors tell their stories about ghost ships, they almost always speak about seeing a lone craft. At least 25 sailors and officers, however, saw a small convoy of ghost warships in 1963. "We didn't just see them," recalled Ed Pelten, "we sailed right through their formation."

Pelten's ship encountered light fog in the mid-Atlantic about 5:00 a.m. the day of the incident. "We could see what looked like about a dozen ships ahead of us through the patches of fog," he said.

Pelten, a cook's helper at the time, had just brought coffee to the wheelhouse when the lookout called out the presence of the ships dead ahead, and sailing in their direction. The radar operator hadn't raised a blip on his screen, however.

"I don't know if the officer in charge had a sixth sense about those ships or if he was just stupid," Pelten said. "He didn't reduce speed or change course. He just sailed right for them."

Although he claims the ships looked solid and real, there was no collision as they steamed into the formation. "We ended up right in the middle of them all. There were ships all around us, or at least they looked like ships. Real close too. But all of a sudden they were gone—disappeared. Nobody said anything. We just looked at each other and things got back to normal, sort of."

Someday perhaps scientists will be able to explain exactly what those images are that appear mysteriously, linger just long enough to cast fear and wonder into the minds of sailors, and then vanish as strangely as they came.

—*Richard Bauman,*
West Covina, Calif.

Angels Have Wheels

Have you ever had one of those days when it was so hot outside that you found it was hard to breathe, and you could not find any relief from the heat? It was a day like this in the summer of 1948. I was only 18 years old, and the Air Force had assigned me to an air base in Roswell, New Mexico. I know that this is the time when the ship from outer space was supposed to have crashed near Roswell. But this is not a story about space ships, or little green men. This is a story about a young man who was away from home for the first time, and was very lonely.

I had always been very interested in caves and caverns, so I became very happy when I found out that I would get my first weekend pass. I wanted to visit the Carlsbad Caverns. As it was a very hot day, I put on my summer uniform and hitchhiked rides to Carlsbad. The caverns were everything I had hoped they would be. I had planned to start back to the base as soon as I came out of the caverns, but instead I found that the town was very interesting also. I had lunch, then walked around town looking in some of the souvenir shops. It was late by the time I started to hitchhike back to the base.

After a while, a man in an old truck stopped and asked me where I was going. I told him that I was going to the air base in Roswell. He told me to get in and he would give me a ride. After about an hour, he pulled off to the side of the road, and told me that this is where he would have to let me off, but that I should not have a hard time getting another ride, because usually there is a lot of traffic on this road. It was starting to get cold, since the sun went down, and I found myself in the desert without a jacket, or anything else to help me keep warm. This was bad, but I soon found out that it would get worse, because a sandstorm started up. Cars coming just passed me by because they could not see me standing on the side of the road. Now I was not only cold, but also had sand all over me. There was only one thing that I could do. I asked God to please help me to find a ride.

Just after I asked God for help, a car pulled up. A man was driving the car and asked me to get in. He put the heater on high, and asked me where I was going. I told him, and he drove me up to the gate of the base.

After thanking him, I walked up to the gate. The guard on duty asked me where I was coming from at that time of night with just a summer uniform. I told him what had happened, and he told me that he was watching the road, and did not see any cars pull up to the gate. He could not understand why I was walking down the road, and how I got there.

I know that angels are supposed to have wings. But my angel had wheels.

—*Thomas Jacobsen,*
Grant Park, Ill.

Ghost Buggy

Sometimes strange things can happen out in the country that simply defy explanation. Haunting experiences can crop up just about anywhere, I would imagine. I can't reveal the names of the individuals who witnessed these unusual events. They're very private people and simply wouldn't want the publicity of their names being used. But I can assure you that they are very honest and reliable people.

One of them experienced a strange incident while plowing some county roads after a blizzard. He had been doing snowplowing for a lot of years, and usually tried to get out on the job shortly after the snow quit. That is what he was doing that particular night. He had his thermos of coffee and some sandwiches with him, and decided to stay out as late as it took to get the roads cleared of snow.

It was after midnight, and he was plowing the snowdrifts on a quiet country road when he saw the light bobbing ahead of him. As he got closer, he rubbed his eyes to make sure he wasn't seeing things. But there, out in the windy chill of a Minnesota winter night, with the temperatures dropping to zero and the wind-chill factor much colder yet, he saw a one-horse buggy. It was coming up opposite to him, and he slowed down his snowplow to get a better look.

The horse was coming through the deep snow with little effort. There was steam blowing from its nostrils. A lantern hung just above the invisible driver and below the roof of the buggy. It was too dark in the interior of the buggy to see the face of the driver. But he could see gloved hands extending out into the light, holding on to the reins. The buggy went by him before he could study it much longer, and he just sat in his snowplow in total bewilderment.

He looked out his rear window and saw the lantern light vanish in the swirling snow. He continued working, but was shaken by this strange old buggy. He knew all the people in this part of the county. None of them owned a horse, let alone an old-fashioned buggy. Besides, who could possibly be foolish enough to be out after midnight on a cold, stormy night? Was the apparition a ghost? A warp in time?

One thing is certain, country doctors used to make house calls even in blizzards if there was an emergency back in the horse-and-buggy days. Perhaps it was a country doctor braving the storm to help a sick patient—who suddenly crossed a time zone into the future. Or perhaps it was the ghost of one of these doctors who perished on a mission of mercy on a winter night so long ago.

—Tom R. Kovach,
Park Rapids, Minn.

Vanishing Truck

In 1972, when I was about 18, a very strange and unexplainable thing happened to me. I was returning home one night after work at around 11:00 when I happened upon an old truck on my side of the road. The truck was stopped and was running. This was on an old country road that had no streetlights and was very desolate.

The truck looked exactly like the one my next-door neighbor owned: an old, faded red truck with wooden slats in the back. My neighbor was an elderly gentleman, and the first thought that occurred to me was that he had had a heart attack, or was sick in some way.

I pulled up in front of the truck, maybe 10 or 15 feet away, to see if I could help him. I got out of the car, and as I was walking around to the front, the truck vanished!

I was stunned for a moment. Then I walked up to where it had been parked. There was a ring of fire on the ground about three feet in diameter. I stood there until the fire went out. Then I got back in my car and tried to find the truck, but it was nowhere to be seen.

The next day I went back to that spot. On the ground was a black ring of a charcoal-like substance where the fire had been. The only explanation I have is that it was a UFO in disguise.

By the way, my neighbor was fine, and I did not share the incident with him. I will never forget that night.

—*Marsha Bass,*
Goodlettsville, Tenn.

Angels on the Highway

This is the true account of a strange event that happened to my husband's family. On a warm August night in 1994, Angelo Castelonia and his family were driving home after a fun evening of watching the races at Orange County Speedway in Middletown, New York. It was about quarter to one and everyone was very tired.

While driving up Wurtsboro Mountain on Route 17, the dashboard lights suddenly began to dim. The alternator of the 1978 Dodge Aspen was going bad. Hoping they could make it the 18 miles home, they pushed the car to its limit and it finally died about 15 miles from their destination.

Angelo decided he would have to walk home to get the other car. He would have hitched a ride, but at that time of night, there was no one around. He set off, taking his oldest son John with him. His wife Dorothy and their two younger children Jason and Pam stayed in the car. After walking about a quarter of a mile, John pointed to a car that was reversing down the highway toward them. Neither of them had seen or heard the car pass them, but at that point, they really didn't care.

The silver car stopped a few yards away, and as they approached it, the passenger door swung open. They could hear the radio playing the song "I'll Be There." When they reached the car, a model neither of them had ever seen, a pleasant man with a bright pink face and fluffy white hair leaned over and said, "Hi! You two look like you could use a ride. I'm only going as far as Monticello, but I can drop you at Exit 104."

Angelo and John looked at one another for a long moment before speaking. Exit 104 was exactly where they wanted to go. Finally, Angelo said, "Well, that's perfect. You see, we live right across from Monticello Raceway."

"Hop in, then. By the way, my name is Frank Quinn. I'm pleased to meet you."

"Angelo Castelonia here, and this is my son, John. We broke down about a quarter of a mile back. My wife and other two kids are still with my car."

"Well there's no sense leaving them on this dangerous road when I could just swing around and pick them up. I'll turn around at this exit and take you all home at the same time. How's that?"

In what seemed like no time, Frank was letting the other three get into the car. About 25 minutes later, Frank pulled into their driveway. After everyone else had thanked Frank and gone into the house, Angelo said, "Listen, I really appreciate your help; there aren't too many people around here that would have done what you did. Please, let me give you something for your trouble." He pulled a $20 bill from his wallet.

"Nonsense." Frank said. "If you really want to repay me, all you have to do is stop and help the next person you see stranded on the side of the road."

"You know, Frank," Angelo said as he got out of the car, "you really must be my Guardian Angel."

"Maybe I am. Someday I'll meet you at the Silver Fox Golf Club and we'll play a round or two—on me, of course." Having said that, the pink-faced, white-haired man shook his hand and pulled out of the drive. "I'll Be There" was still playing when he left. Angelo turned to wave, but there was no sign of Frank or the quiet silver sedan.

Several months later, Angelo decided to take Frank up on his offer of golf. He looked in the phone book for the address of the golf club in White Lake, but couldn't find a listing. Thinking that was a little strange, he called information and got the same result. Later that day, he was telling a good friend about the encounter with Frank and not being able to find an address for the club.

His friend gave him a very strange look and said, "The Silver Fox burned to the ground way back in 1937. A big housing development stands there now."

Could Frank Quinn have really been a guardian angel? Is it possible he died in that fire and is now watching over others? Unless we see Frank again and ask him, I guess we'll never know.

—*Jennifer Champlain,*
Glen Wild, N.Y.

Right Place, Wrong Time

On July 6, 2004, my mum, Joan Hartley, and myself were walking through the common in Tunbridge Wells in Kent, England, on our way to the local garden center with my three-year-old Alsatian, Lee, who was happily sniffing out and chasing rabbits.

All was well and we were immersed deep in conversation when suddenly Lee began to get very agitated. His ears and tail dropped, his fur prickled along his spine, and he began to whimper and cry around my legs. Sensing his fear, I bent down and reassured him, at the same time remarking to my mum at how quiet it had become. There was no bird song in the woods, something you tend to take for granted, but miss if it isn't there. There was no rustling of leaves, nor even the distant rumble of traffic on the main London road; in fact, there suddenly seemed to be a complete absence of any sound.

Putting Lee back on his lead, we continued on our journey, following a well-worn path. But as we rounded a corner, we were forced to stop and stare in disbelief, for there, not 15 feet in front of us and perched on a large outcrop of rock, stood a large, two-story, red-brick house with three tall chimneys.

Both Mum and I stared in disbelief as neither of us had seen the house before and yet we had both used this path many times before as children and adults.

After the initial shock had worn off, curiousity set in. Where had the mysterious house come from? It certainly wasn't newly built.

Assuming the house to be empty, we decided to take a closer look. Hanging on tight to a still-whimpering Lee, we crept slowly up the garden path and peered through the window. There were crisp net curtains at the windows and several pieces of heavy, old-fashioned furniture inside, but above all there was a really strong smell of beeswax polish and carbolic soap, which Mum instantly recognized from her childhood.

Not wanting to be caught trespassing on the property, Mum and I slipped away quickly and continued our journey, our conversation now on the newly discovered house. Mum remarked that although it had been raining heavily the night before and the common was, to quote her words, "quite soggy underfoot," both the garden and path of the house were perfectly dry.

Returning from the garden center, plants in hand, we decided to pay the mysterious house another visit, but even though we traced our steps to the exact spot, there was no sign of the new house, just the large outcrop of now-empty rock.

A few months after the incident, we were talking to a group of friends about what had happened when an elderly man who had obviously overheard our conversation told us that the house we described had indeed stood there many years ago. It was called Romanoff Lodge and was occupied during the war by White Russians before it had been turned into a children's home. Sadly, he could provide us with no further information on it, but he did tell us another story about something he and his wife had seen.

Mr. and Mrs. Williams of Grove Hill Rise, Tunbridge Wells, Kent, were out for a picnic one day in Speldhurst, again in Tunbridge Wells, back in the summer of 1983, when suddenly they heard a strange whirling noise and muffled voices. Deciding to investigate, they walked up the hill and gazed down onto an old-fashioned working farm, complete with a water wheel, horses pulling hay carts, and people working in the next field wearing smocks and forking the hay.

Both watched the scene for several minutes until it began to fade and be replaced once more by the road that should have been there and the normal summer field.

So where did the mysterious house and farm scene come from? Or perhaps more precisely, where did they go?

—*Jacki Dawson,*
Tunbridge Wells, Kent, England

10

Vortexes, Time Slips, and Portals to Other Dimensions

The stories in this chapter takes us farther from traditional ghost stories than we have yet gone. However, if we are open to the existence of ghosts, spirits, and an unseen world, we must consider possibilities stranger yet.

Certain locations seem to be focal points for paranormal phenomena. Some of these are recognized as sacred sites, others are just considered weird. "Vortex" is one term used to describe such places.

Seekers of the strange and numinous flock to such areas as Sedona, Arizona, or California's High Desert, just as pilgrims have traveled to holy sites for thousands of years. These places, it is said, have an unusual energy, somehow more conducive to travel between worlds and visionary experiences.

Among the phenomena reported at vortexes is a disruption in the normal flow of time: "time slips" or "time warps." Portals to other dimensions may open at random, generating unpredictable activity in their surroundings. Witnesses may catch a glimpse of their location in another time period, or in a parallel universe.

Wild stuff, indeed! Of course, such experiences may be purely subjective, taking place only in the percipient's mind. That does not make them any less fascinating.

Strange Experiences

I experienced many unusual happenings in my early childhood, but paid little attention to them. My first major experience with the unknown was in 1970.

We had just moved to Twentynine Palms, California, which back then was little more than one stop sign along the highway in the middle of the Mojave Desert. From the 1950s to the mid-'80s this area was known for sightings and landings of UFOs and for mass outdoor get-togethers of people hoping to meet aliens from outer space at Giant Rock Airport and the Integratron Complex a few miles north of the city of Joshua Tree.

I wasn't aware of the unusual nature of the area, but I was learning fast. People I met were quick to acknowledge that they had seen UFOs. Some expressed joy at being able to paint pictures or write with the help of spiritual guides. Others told stories of sleepwalking in the night and waking up to find that they stood at the foot of a nearby mountain. It seemed almost half the people you talked to in that area in those days had a strange story like this.

Early one spring morning, I awoke alone as the first light of a new day began to show itself through the curtains of my window. I suddenly realized I was totally paralyzed and couldn't move any part of my body. Then at the foot of my bed there appeared a giant circle of psychedelic points of light of all colors of the spectrum. It was like animation light in the real world. A couple seconds later, this wheel of light began to spin in a clockwise direction, first slowly, then faster and faster until the lights began to blend into a single circle.

At the circle's fastest motion of spin, it disappeared and simultaneously a white, cloud-like apparition arose from floor level to about the height of the bed, covering the whole room. It seemed to be coming from a huge wooden door surrounded by clouds located in a corner of the ceiling to my right.

This continued for what I felt was an hour but was actually only a few minutes. It stopped as if someone had turned off a movie projector.

At this point I was sweating as if I had just run a mile and was feeling fatigued as well.

In the days and weeks that followed I considered every aspect of this incident and concluded it was a supernatural event, not an illusion.

The human race is being continuously enlightened by a higher power. I believe that higher power is both extraterrestrial and from the great mind that created all there is, which is God.

—*Tony Elliott,*
San Antonio, Tex.

Strange Encounter in Nature

I am a retired teacher and student of metaphysics. Two years ago, my husband and I moved to a wooded area 20 miles north of Leesburg, a town in central Florida. We'd left a lovely home on a small pond, surrounded by several lakes. Children in the neighborhood swam or fished in the lakes under the shade of old oak trees. A pair of nesting whooping cranes, long on the endangered species list, was often seen in the backyard of a nearby house.

Despite great controversy and much public debate, the city began spraying a potent herbicide from airboats along the shoreline of the lakes. We could not stay and watch as lakes turned into dead zones. Within a month, we had sold our house and moved to a mobile home on a large lot about a mile east of the Ocala National Forest.

After a year of enjoying country life and gardening, we discovered a great place for walking: Sunnyhill Preserve, a mile west of our property. It has about 4,000 acres of woods, meadows, wetlands, and nature trails that border the Oklawaha River. In the fall of 2005, I began walking alone, as my husband's physical disability kept him at home. On this particular fall day, I left home early in the morning for a long-anticipated walk along the levee of the Oklawaha River. Fall brought cooler air and the change of seasons was invigorating— perfect conditions for walking.

The entrance to Sunnyhill is impressive. An old restored farmhouse, under a canopy of ancient oak trees, greets visitors as they drive into the parking lot. Today it was empty except for my car. Enjoying the solitude and privacy, I locked the car and walked to the meadow.

The sky was a huge blue bowl overhead, the grass a green carpet under my feet. I stopped in front of a certain oak tree by the trail not far from the river to pray silently for worldwide preservation of nature. It was a personal ceremony that always lifted my spirits.

I continued on to the levee, feeling lighthearted and adventurous. The river stretched out to the horizon, sparkles of light on the water. A few waterbirds and a lone egret by the bank were my only companions.

Thirty minutes later, I left the levee and headed back to the meadow. The sun was getting higher in the sky and chores at home were not finished. I paused at the same oak tree, expecting to say a short prayer and leave. It was then that an ordinary day became extraordinary.

A dark blue disk appeared over a low branch and hovered there silently. It was the size of a dinner plate and appeared to be inanimate. I stood still, curious and in awe of the phenomenon. Meditating for a calm state of mind, I observed it carefully. It was six or seven yards away, about five feet in the air, opaque, flat, and circular. It stood out clearly in the sunlight, almost like a projection. Could there be a projector in the tree? The absence of mechanical or electrical devices in the area made this theory seem impossible.

After a few minutes of standing, I tried a new tactic. Perhaps contact was possible. I directed my awareness toward the disk as if it were a real entity and mentally requested communication. At that instant, it left the tree branch and sailed smoothly and swiftly across the open space on a direct path to my face. Startled by the quick action, I lost the meditative state and the disk disappeared three feet from me. Bright sunshine and empty space was all that was left of the experience. Who would believe me?

I walked back to the car deep in thought and full of wonderment. This was the beginning of a new adventure. Other paranormal phenomena must exist somewhere in the thousands of acres of Sunnyhill Preserve, just waiting to be explored. Next time I would be braver, less afraid of the unknown, and more willing to allow the experience to continue to its conclusion.

—*Barbara J. Taylor,*
Umatilla, Fla.

Miniature Time Warp

This incident happened in March of this year. I will call it a mini time warp for lack of a better description. I was driving to work on the freeway from the San Fernando Valley to Los Angeles. It was about 9:30 in the morning, and as soon as I got on the freeway, it was bumper-to-bumper, moving about ten miles an hour.

As I got into Burbank, still inching along, I caught something in my peripheral vision. I looked over to my right and saw the Metrolink station. There was a police car parked there. At this point, traffic had come to a complete stop. I was looking at the police car and wondering what was going on. I started fiddling with the radio.

The next thing I remember, I looked up to see that traffic was moving again, and I started moving with it. I looked to my left, and I was two miles behind the train station just coming into Burbank. I went past the grocery stores on my left, and the high-rise buildings, and came up on the Media Center Mall, which is across from the Metrolink station. I thought: *If there's a police car at the train station* . . . I looked to my right, and sure enough there was the police car.

The traffic was moving a little faster, and I drove by thinking, *This is absolutely crazy, almost like the movie* Groundhog Day. I was hoping I wasn't going to look over to my left and find myself coming into Burbank again.

I told my husband about it later that day, but knowing Mr. Prove-it-to-Me, I knew he would come up with some answer. He suggested that when I had been fiddling with the radio, I had taken my eyes off the road, and my foot off the brake, and had been almost coasting by the train station, suggesting movement and making me think that I had driven past it.

I thought about that, but how would that have put me two miles behind, driving back into Burbank? If I had coasted by the station, not really concentrating on where I was, I would have found myself past the station, and two miles ahead. And why did I know about the police car?

It was like having the experience of driving to work, and not remembering anything about the drive—something we here in L.A. experience way too much because of our time on the freeway. But when I found myself coming into Burbank for the second time,

I was very alert and amazed at what was happening. I have never had an experience like this. I think I got caught in a miniature time warp. But then again, this is L.A.

—*Anna Cummins,*
Sun Valley, Calif.

Battle Hymn

As a young boy, I wished more than anything to be a Boy Scout. On my 12th birthday that wish came true, and a couple of years later as a first-class Scout and a patrol leader, I attended a patrol leaders' conference at Snapper Creek Boy Scout Camp on the edge of the Everglades west of Miami, Florida. The leaders of a little less than 100 troops camped around the perimeter of a large parade ground. My troop, Troop 18 from Everglades Elementary School, was equipped with old army surplus tents and just the bare bones of camp equipment. On the other extreme, Troop 1 from Coral Gables had everything: eight-man tents, a field kitchen and dining tent, and even a piano mounted on a trailer.

After supper and the end of the evening's activities of the first night in camp, the scoutmaster of Troop 1 started playing the piano, and his boys sang the songs he played. Soon the boys from other troops started drifting over to Troop 1 and joining in the singing. I was one of them. It was a wonderful experience on a typical warm, muggy night, as campfires flickered all around the open field. Soon there were hundreds of boys singing, and you could feel the magic of the evening growing.

About halfway through the first verse of "Battle Hymn of the Republic," it happened, but apparently only to me. The air suddenly turned cold, and the smell of rotting tropical vegetation became a strong mixture of sweat and manure. I heard noises of men shouting, horses laboring, and wagons creaking. Wheeling around to face the open parade ground, the 70 or 80 small campfires that had been there when I last looked had turned into thousands of flickering campfires as far as the eye could see. Men in uniform, horses, equipment, grimy white tents were everywhere. And then they were gone.

I must have blinked a hundred times at the old familiar scene, and felt the heavy warm air in my lungs as my mouth hung open in disbelief. Sixty years later I can truthfully say that I have experienced many magical evenings, but this is the only truly mystical experience I've ever had. It has haunted me ever since.

—Gene Curry,
Blue Ridge, Ga.

My Strange Birthday Gift

Eventually, things come full circle, and so it was when my childhood friend Cindy and I were reunited at a high school reunion planning meeting. At one of the sites we were considering for our alumni reunion picnic, something very strange occurred. I started getting chills and shivers throughout my entire body. It was summer, and the temperature was a warm 80 degrees. Cindy looked at me with a puzzled expression and asked, "Are you cold?"

I smiled.

Until then, I had not shared with my friend that my hobby and passion is ghost hunting. I broached the subject by explaining that the chills I was experiencing indicated the presence of a ghost. In fact, this particular ghost was now walking right beside us. Naturally, Cindy was a little stunned and wanted to know more.

We discussed how spirits often draw energy (heat) from us and from the surrounding area. Those of us who are sensitive enough to feel this energy pull will experience chills and be able to feel cold spots in houses and even outdoors.

I also thought it only fair to tell my friend that I am a real live "ghost magnet." Spirits are attracted to me. I warned her that this was the first of many strange occurrences she might expect while being with me. She might even see me disappear from this dimension.

Months passed, and my good friend and I made plans for an outing to celebrate my upcoming December birthday. However, on my birthday, we completely changed our original plans. I believe that this is relevant due to what occurred later that day.

On my birthday, the weather was cold but nice, so we decided it would be fun to take a drive through Amish Country. We grabbed the appropriate wraps, and Cindy pulled on a pair of warm gloves. She suggested that we go to an indoor flea market and eat at the Amish restaurant next door. However, upon reaching our destination, we found the flea market and restaurant closed.

Cindy suggested that we reinstate our original plans and go to the restaurant that we had first chosen. It was a bit out of our way, but the weather was good and there was still plenty of time. We debated the route—interstate or scenic? Scenic won, and we were again on our way for my birthday treat.

There was very little traffic on the back road, so I was able to drive at the posted speed limit of 45 miles per hour. As we were driving, I noticed a stately old Victorian house on the left side of the street.

"Hey Cindy, look to your left at this beautiful house."

Immediately past the house, there was an intersection with no traffic lights and no stop signs. As we approached the intersection, I saw a car coming toward us. In fact, we were the only two cars on the road. As the car approached, it came so close that I could see the driver's face. Cindy was still looking at the old house.

Suddenly, the driver of the other car made a left turn—right in front of us! I kept my car under control and tried to avoid broadsiding the other car. I slammed on the brakes and hit the horn. The driver of the other car continued at the same slow pace—turning directly into our path.

By quickly steering to the left, I avoided hitting the car broadside, but I knew we would surely clip its rear end. Then, a weird thing happened. Cindy and I saw my car pass directly through the other one. Instinctively, we both listened for the crunch, but there was no impact whatsoever. We were in awe at what had just taken place. Did my car really go through the other car? Why was the driver totally unaware?

Cindy and I did not talk for quite some time after this happened. We were both stunned. Finally, Cindy broke the silence.

"Lorraine, remember what you told me about yourself? I think you transported us into another dimension! And where are my gloves? They were on my hands, and now they are gone!"

I believe that Cindy was correct. I drove us into another dimension to avoid a collision. On that beautiful December day, I was granted the very strangest and best birthday gift of all. Was this miraculous, life-saving event all my doing or was it a gift from the universe?

—*Lorraine A. Scott,*
Seven Hills, Ohio

A Rip in Time

One Saturday night I was on my way home. I had left a busy town and started down the main highway. All of a sudden the sky went completely black, then all traffic and sound stopped. My friend and I found ourselves on the highway alone. She noticed the dark before I did.

"Hey, where did all the stars go?" She looked through the car window.

"I don't know." I stared upward. "I saw a full moon when we left town. I guess it's clouding up."

We decided to turn on the car radio, but we only got static. We proceeded on home without even seeing a cat or wild animal along the country road. We arrived home; everything was still, dark, and quiet. It was beginning to become spooky. My cat, who is always waiting on the porch for me, wasn't anywhere to be seen.

After several hours the stars came out. The cat appeared on the porch as if by magic, and then traffic started going up the road. I checked my watch only to find out it had stopped.

Spooky, you say; but that's not the whole story yet.

Several years later, when I had tried to push that odd occurence out of my mind, I was at my sister's house with a different friend. It was a Wednesday night around 9:00. Right in the middle of a busy city, all noise stopped and the sky went totally dark. Again, my friend was the one to say something first. I hadn't said anything to her about my other weird experience.

Oh no, not again, I thought. I decided to go on with what I was doing, hoping everything would soon return to normal. The little house dog was shivering, pacing up and down the hallway. His hair was standing up on his back. I opened the door for him to go out, but he bolted back into the house as if a pack of wolves was chasing him. I followed him back to the bedroom. "Come here, I thought you wanted to go outside." I reached for him, but his eyes were red as fire, and he growled. I backed away and let him alone.

I looked outside again. The streetlights were on, but there was no light in the sky. Only black, no cars, no noise, not even the sound of a pin drop. I like quiet, but this was right-out-of-this-world quiet. A strange presence hung over the house. You couldn't put your finger on it, but it was like when some people say they can feel evil.

We decided to go outside and face whatever was happening head-on. We sat on the front porch hoping to see some sign of life. After several hours had passed the stars came out. We heard a siren, and then traffic began. We went back inside the house; the creepy feeling was gone, and the dog came up to us wagging his tail. He went outside.

I now knew it wasn't my imagination. The weird happening had just occurred again. The dog sensed it, and my friend noticed it. What a relief to know I wasn't alone! But my friend didn't want to talk about it.

Well, it happened, and it's over, I thought. *I'll just try to forget it.*

Have you ever tried to forget something like that? Well, it just stays in your memory.

"When have you had a quiet night here in town?" I asked my sister when she returned.

"Never," she replied. "Not in the time we've lived here. There's always something going on."

When people see UFOs at least they can take a picture, but in this case, what's there to take a picture of?

Well, you guessed it: it happened again, this time at 8:00 on a Saturday night. I was at home. There was traffic, dogs barking, airplanes going overhead, and owls hooting. I was outside in my lawn chair enjoying the night when the moon disappeared. The sky went black, and all the animal sounds stopped. I looked to see the time. Oh no, my watch had stopped also. Right up the road a racetrack had already started the race. The noise was extremely loud, but then there was complete silence. It was as if all life had just frozen. But why do I go on with life, as does anyone I'm with?

I tried to carry on and stay busy. I figured everything would return to normal soon as it had always done before. Wrong. This time the quiet, dark, and spooky feeling kept on and on. I sat in my lawn chair, read, and talked to my mother for what seemed like a week. We tried the TV, but we couldn't seem to get any channel, only static and a few words we couldn't understand. I guess we might have gone crazy if not for books, each other, and the fact that we finally went to bed. We tried to sleep, but it was too quiet. We got up several times to find it was still dark and quiet. I was beginning to wonder if I would ever see the light, or hear some kind of sound again.

I wondered if it was like a ballgame: three strikes and you're out. I looked over at the clock one more time. The battery clock read 2:00 p.m. The event didn't seem to have bothered it. But the electric clock read 5:00 a.m. That was a nine-hour difference in the clocks.

I looked out one more time hoping for at least some light. I was tired of the dark, quiet, and spooky feeling. I noticed blue light outside. Thank heavens, it was at least becoming daylight. I heard a chirp of a bird, then a car passed. The eerie feeling had faded away too.

Several days later I asked a neighbor if they noticed how quiet it was Saturday night. They laughed and said, "You must be talking about some other night. That night was so noisy we hardly got a wink of sleep. The racetrack went on until 1:00 a.m., then the traffic tore up the road after." I never said any more. How could I live a few houses away from them and experience total quiet, while they had an unbearably noisy night?

I checked the clocks out later. The electric one was with the TV and radio. But the battery one was also three days ahead of the time of month it was. Which one do you believe? The most logical one would be the electric one. But I know the event went on for what seemed like forever.

I don't know what to call this strange paranormal event, but I hope I never experience it again. What force is out there, and what triggers it? If I knew what to do to untrigger it, I would.

—*Margaret Worley,*
Watertown, Tenn.

Night Becomes Day

I will never forget the experience of that night. I believe it happened in the summer of 1966. My friend Marty Brown and I were outside in the backyard with my telescope. With a chart in hand, we would gaze at the night sky, in search of planets, stars, and constellations.

One evening something streaked past us. Strange, too low for a shooting star. It came from the southeast, shot over us, and descended to the northeast. We heard a loud explosion. Suddenly the night sky became day.

I can still see it after all these years. It was in slow motion. We actually saw the sun rise. Stars just disappeared. Then the sun set and the stars reappeared. We stared at each other in disbelief. Then we ran to tell my parents, who promptly told us that our imaginations had gotten the better of us.

For days after that I searched the paper for an answer. Nothing.

What was it? Oh, I have my theories, but no concrete explanations.

To this day I still observe the sky with my telescope. And yes, I have seen other strange things, but not like that night in 1966.

—*Mary Holly,*
Fraser, Mich.

Mystery of Two Guns

It was late May 1972 and my friend Gary and I decided to take a road trip. We would head out to the West Coast, then back through Colorado to our hometown of St. Louis.

Our route took us through Oklahoma to Amarillo, Texas, where we spent the first night at a KOA campground. Then we traveled through New Mexico to Flagstaff, Arizona, where we spent the second night.

It was our passage through New Mexico and Arizona that still has me perplexed nearly 34 years later. We left Amarillo at about 9:00 a.m. and reached the New Mexico border around 10:00. About ten miles into New Mexico we saw a billboard, the biggest one I have ever seen. It was so close to the highway that you could spit out the window and hit it. It had a yellow background with red lettering and read: "Visit Two Guns, Arizona. Home of the 1999 World's Fair."

I thought it was an odd billboard.

Another ten miles later we saw another one that read the same: "Visit Two Guns, Arizona. Home of the 1999 World's Fair."

Gary and I began to wonder about the town of Two Guns and we checked our travel map.

There it was, about 25 miles west of Winslow, Arizona, but it looked so small. We wondered how such a small town could host a World's Fair 27 years into the future.

In all, we saw about two dozen of these giant billboards, spaced about ten miles apart throughout the state of New Mexico. Again, they were so tall that the last one we passed blocked out the sun, which was high in the sky at 2:00 p.m.

Then we hit the Arizona border and saw no more billboards. We spent the afternoon touring the Painted Desert, then continued across Arizona into the early evening, but saw no more billboards. Now we were wondering why we saw all those signs in New Mexico but not one in Arizona. We passed through Winslow about 8:00 p.m., and finally around 8:30 we saw what we had been looking forward to for hours. We passed a little sign that read "Two Guns"; no population, just "Two Guns."

We looked to our right and saw scrub brush and mesas as far as we could see. We looked to our left and saw the same. No city lights, no buildings, no stop light or stop sign, no seedy bar, no greasy spoon diner, and no grubby service station. We were in the middle of nowhere and all we saw was an abandoned shack on the south side of I-40 where the town was supposed to be, according to the map. That's it!

Well, we busted out laughing. We thought it was pretty funny seeing all those signs advertising a non-existent town and an event too far into the future for anyone to care, let alone remember. For the rest of our trip through Arizona, Nevada, California, Utah, Colorado, and on to St. Louis we made jokes about visiting Two Guns, Arizona: "Home of the 1999 World's Fair."

Two weeks after we returned, my roommates Steve and Don decided to take a road trip to California to visit our pal Phil who had recently transferred there. They took the exact same route that Gary and I did. I told Steve about the billboards and told him to look for them, although it was impossible to miss them.

Ten days later they returned and Steve entered the nightclub that he played for as a musician.

It was Friday night about 9:00 and Steve had to play right away. When Steve reached his first set break, I asked him about the signs. Weren't they a hoot?

"What signs?" asked Steve.

"You know, the ones about Two Guns!"

"I didn't see them."

I was shocked. "How could you not see them? They were huge and right next to the highway."

"There were no signs of any kind," he assured me.

Well, I didn't know what to say so I let the subject drop.

For the next 34 years I would occasionally think about those billboards. I knew there was nothing logical about what we saw. Then in June 2006 I mentioned the incident to family members at a graduation party while discussing paranormal events. We all concluded that I should contact the state of Arizona to find out more about Two Guns, which I did.

It turns out that Two Guns is on a national register of ghost towns. It was built as a tourist stop in the late 1800s for people visiting Canyon Diablo just to the north. Additional amenities were added in the 1930s, and at its height had quite a few buildings, including a hotel, a food emporium, and a zoo. It died out in the 1940s when I-40 was built. The remnants of the town can easily be seen from the interstate.

This presents a second problem about that day in 1972. When Gary and I passed by Two Guns, there was nothing visible but a wooden shack. There was no intersection to turn at to go to the town.

So, we saw billboards that we should not have seen and we did not see the town we should have seen. Also, the signs were gone two weeks later when my roomies passed through.

I suspect that Gary and I stepped into the "twilight zone" that day in May 1972. We may have gone through a time shift and passed through at a time before the town was built. I have had this happen to me twice more since then, but that is another story and not nearly as interesting as this one.

Perhaps this event was nothing more than a big cosmic joke perpetrated by beings from the heavenly realm, or some other dimension, at the expense of Gary and I. They probably had a good laugh, as did we.

—*Larry Hammelman,*
Defiance, Mo.

The Fan People

Back in the mid-1990s, my wife Cheryl and I lived in a small country house near Perry, Florida. The house was quite old, but had just been moved from its original site to a five-acre lot.

Although the house was on a dirt road and was not very close to the other houses, one of our neighbors kept hunting dogs in a pen behind the house. The dogs barked all hours of the day and night.

Rather than confront the neighbors, we would usually turn on the fan to the central heating and cooling system. The system had been salvaged from a much larger house, and it made quite a breeze. It also generated a considerable amount of white noise that masked the sound of the dogs.

While my wife has believed in ghosts and spirits since she was a young girl, I am a skeptic. My wife has claimed to have seen and felt ghosts before, but I always believed that she was just dreaming or letting her imagination run away with her.

One evening, after my wife had already gone to sleep, I was lying awake in bed when I heard what sounded like two men and a woman talking right outside our bedroom window. I couldn't quite make out the words, but the voices sounded just like three people having a friendly conversation. At first, I was puzzled; then I was angry. I couldn't see why anyone would be talking outside our window, since the house was set back about 100 feet from the road. So I peered through the blinds and looked outside. Even though I could still hear people talking, I saw no one. I then quietly opened the bedroom window and stuck my head outside. The only sound I heard was from the crickets.

This episode repeated itself on several other occasions. Once I even got dressed and went outside to look. The voices generally seemed to be either two men and a woman, or one man and one woman. Although I didn't hear the voices most nights, I finally decided that the sounds were somehow caused by air traveling through the ducts, and gave up worrying about it.

One evening, just before going to bed, my wife asked me if I had heard the "fan people." I asked her what she was talking about. She answered, half expecting me to laugh at her, "The voices when the fan is turned on."

I was flabbergasted. I had no idea she heard the voices too. "You mean the two men and the woman?" I asked.

"Yes, and sometimes it is one man and a woman," she replied. It turned out that we had both been hearing the voices for some time.

Over time, the voices came with less and less frequency. Eventually, they stopped altogether. Before they stopped, my wife claimed to have heard them once when the fan was off. We did have a few other unusual occurrences in the house, but never felt frightened or threatened.

Before we moved, my wife had a friend who was psychic visit the house. According to this friend, when the house was moved it had been placed on the pathway to another dimension. The house itself wasn't haunted, but spirits would frequently pass by it on their way to the afterlife.

Do I believe this? I'm not sure. I will, however, admit to being much more open-minded to the possibility that ghosts are real.

—*David Hoes,*
Clermont, Fla

11

Past-Life Memories

Reincarnation, a concept associated with Eastern religion and philosophy, is commonly understood to refer to a process by which an individual soul is reborn in a new body after the physical death of a previous incarnation. According to Hindu and Buddhist teachings, the process of spiritual evolution ends with enlightenment and release from the cycle of death and rebirth.

The concept of reincarnation has been used to explain what appear to be memories of past lives. Details of a previous existence may arise consciously in response to scenes or artifacts of the past, in unusually vivid dreams, or through guided meditation or hypnosis.

A somewhat more subtle view of reincarnation holds that individual souls do not actually transmigrate into new bodies, because individual existence is itself an illusion. In conformity with this outlook, past-life memories would have to be explained as somehow tapping into the collective memory-bank of human consciousness.

Either way, past-life memories are often surprisingly detailed and experienced with visceral intensity.

The Dream

I was marching in a column of a very large body of Roman soldiers, near the edge of the trees in what seemed to be a large forest.

Without any warning the forest came alive. We were being attacked by forces I could not see. I could hear the screams and the shouts of those around me. Then I was on the edge of the woods being forced down the sloping ground. Fighting was raging all around me as barbarian warriors, some painted, poured out of the trees and engaged the Roman legionaries.

Groups of soldiers were pushed farther and farther down the hillside and split up into ever-smaller groups. The noise and mayhem were everywhere. The barbarians, it seemed, had the upper hand, swinging large axes and swords.

I found myself not far from the edge of the trees. I was exhausted and could no longer fight. My arms were unable to move, and I realized that I had no helmet. Had I lost it in the fighting, or had it been knocked off my head earlier in the woods?

I found a small hollow in the ground and knelt down in it. At this point I became aware of another Roman legionary standing about six feet away from me. As I looked up at him, I heard this whooshing sound and saw the end of a sword decapitate him. In slow motion, I watched the head fall to the ground, still in its helmet. It bounced a few times and came to rest not far from the body.

I wondered how long it would be before the barbarians found my hiding place. As this thought was going through my head, I heard once more that same whooshing noise, then everything went black.

The dream ended.

For my birthday in 2000, I received the book *In Quest of the Lost Legions* by Retired Major T. Clunn, MBE. Upon reading this book, I knew instantly that here was the actual site of my dream years before. I wrote to the publishers and the author. This in turn led my wife and me to visit Germany with the author, but one more piece of amazing information was to reach me before this trip was made.

Here I will quote from the actual letter I received concerning a site at Kalkreise near Osnabruck in Germany: "In the area of the last part of the engagement were found the remains of two Legionaries, one was headless, the skull lying off to one side and the skull of the other soldier neatly cleaved down the middle." Just as I had witnessed in my dream, some ten years before!

The actual event took place in AD 9 when the Roman governor Q. Varus lost three legions, the 17th, the 18th, and the 19th, in the forests of northern Germany to the German tribal leader Arminius. Here was proof, at least in some manner.

Later I was taken to the spot in Kalkreise where the remains had been found lying in the soil. Was this where I had perished some 2,000 years before? I threw a bunch of wildflowers into the spot and said a prayer.

One evening shortly after my return from Germany, a friend who was also interested in Roman history asked me if I wished to take part in a television program. I said I might and asked him what it was about. To my amazement, he told me that Channel 4 was making a program about the Varus event in Germany in AD 9.

Shortly afterward I found myself dressed as a Roman legionary, killed again high on a hillside in a dense forest. History was indeed repeating itself—but this time I lived on, thankfully, after death.

In June 2003 I was invited to return to Kalkreise, where both German and Roman history reenactors were taking part in a show on the actual site of the battle. Again I found myself dressed as a Roman soldier, standing in the same spot among the trees close to the camp of Arminius.

On the second day of the event at Kalkreise, I was speaking with a man who told me about a conversation he had with a woman and her son who had come from Iceland to visit the site. They had been walking up in the wooded area close to the spot of my experience when the woman turned to her son and asked, "Can you see what I am seeing?"

"No," he replied. "I do not see anything other than the trees."

The woman then informed him that she could see the figure of a Roman soldier wearing armor, but only from the waist up, looking out from the trees in their direction. This ghostly figure was close to where the remains of the two soldiers had been found lying in the soil.

Finally I paid a visit to the newly opened museum at Kalkreise, where I found myself looking at the remains of the skeleton that Major T. Clunn informed me might have been one of those in my dream experience.

Indeed, it was most weird to be standing in that darkened section within the museum, looking at what may have been my own mortal remains from another lifetime. As I gazed, I wondered about the new science of DNA testing. Could this throw any light into my possible earlier existence?

I would also wish to discover if I knew the soldier standing close by me who was decapitated. Is this person within the circle of those I know today? Could a past-life therapist provide more insight? Had I somehow re-entered some dimensional doorway to the past, a gateway to another time? Did I actually travel through space and time?

Sometime in 2004 I was to find myself transported back to those dark forests of northern Germany. Again, without warning, I found myself standing among the trees. I could not see or hear any other soldiers close to my position. I was dressed in the armor of a Roman legionary. Some distance away was a group of about six Roman auxiliary soldiers huddled together. I could see their chain mail and bronze helmets. They seemed to be talking very quietly. At this point something like my inner sense told me not to move or disturb them. I felt they were plotting or up to no good. I recall as I stood there silently watching them that I strained to hear their voices but could not, and if I moved from my position behind the tree they would quickly fall upon me. Then, as I stood there, it ended and I was back home in this time.

—*John S. Richardson,*
Fife, United Kingdom

Have I Lived Before?

I was born on a farm during the horse-and-buggy days, but I never drove the team, or had anything to do with the horses. Only my father and grandfather used the horses.

When I was about 12 years old, a relative gave us a horse. I wanted to keep it, but Grandfather said, "No, we do not have room or feed for a third horse."

Then Mother said, "Grandmother can use the horse."

With only a rope around the horse's head, I led her to a porch and jumped on, bareback. It was a moment I will never forget. I felt as if I had been riding all my life. I felt like I was part of the horse as I rode the mile to Grandmother's farm, guiding the horse with the rope and my legs against her sides. This unbelievable familiarity baffled me, because I had never heard of reincarnation. It would be many years before I would learn about it and become interested in the possibility of past lives.

Forty-three years later, I began collecting firing replicas of muzzleloading, black powder guns of the style popular in the Old West. I bought a Derringer, a pepperbox, a flintlock, and a replica of the 1860 Colt with a seven-and-a-half inch barrel, which was used by both the North and South during the Civil War. I learned that sheriffs and gunfighters did not use this Colt—the long barrel took too long to come out of a holster during "fast-draw" combat. Instead, they used the "Sheriff's model" 1860, with a barrel that was two inches shorter.

I decided to add the "Sheriff's model" to my collection. It was delivered by UPS. I was so anxious to see it, I unpacked it in my van—and got the surprise of my life!

My hand closed over the grip, and I drew it instinctively, fanning the hammer with the palm of my left hand. For a few seconds, my van disappeared, and I was in a gunfight! I did not see my opponent—my view ahead was clouded, as if through a veil.

It lasted only seconds, but I was sure I had held this gun before. It fit my hand like a glove. Fanning the hammer with the left hand was a common practice in those days. These were single-action guns, and there was no time to cock the hammer during fast-draw combat. Being the first to fire was more important than accuracy, because the second shot, by fanning, was immediate.

I have no idea on which side of the law I had been, if this was indeed a flashback from a previous life.

Even today, many years after the experience, I feel an inexplicable sensation when I pick up this special gun. It fits my hand as if it belongs. Nothing like this happens when I pick up any other gun.

—*Joseph Kerska,*
Brisbane, Calif.

My Soul Cried Out

While I am not a very religious person, I will always believe in reincarnation because of a powerful experience I had when I was 12 years old. I went to a large airplane show with my father and grandfather. I had no more interest in airplanes or in history than any other average kid my age. Neither my father nor my grandfather is a military veteran.

On the day that we attended, there was a reenactment of a World War II air battle. Planes were painted with the colors and insignia of Allied and Axis air forces. The pilots performed mock dogfights, firing blanks and exploding fireworks that imitated bombs. On a bandstand in the center of the park, three veterans who had been pilots in the war narrated the action over the PA system.

At first, I watched the reenactment with the limited interest of a 12-year-old kid. Suddenly an overwhelming feeling of outrage came over me. I immediately knew that I deserved to be where those three old men were sitting. I deserved to be honored and tell of my deeds in the war. But I could not, because I was trapped in the body of a child. It was as though some hidden side of my personality asserted itself without any warning.

I could barely contain my anger—anger that made no sense for a 12-year-old to feel. I wanted so badly to climb up on stage and start talking about my World

War II experiences—experiences of which I had no conscious memory.

My anger and envy continued until the reenactment ended. I slowly calmed down, but I was left with the absolute certainty that I had lived before. I know beyond any doubt that I was in the war and that my past life was cut short there.

While I have never had another experience as powerful as that one, during my time in the military many things filled me with a strong sense of déjà vu that suggested I remembered aspects of that past life.

—*Jeff Cooper,*
Milwaukee, Wis.

Train Ride To . . . Where?

I am 43 years old, and among the many things that have always fascinated me are reincarnation, astral projection, OOBEs, ghosts and hauntings, UFOs . . . actually anything to do with the paranormal. I've never actually seen a ghost, but I do have firsthand experience with reincarnation.

When I was three or four years old, I kept telling my mom that I remembered riding on a train. I described the scenery to her, how it was hot and dusty. I was wearing a plain brown dress with a bonnet. On my feet I wore ugly brown leather shoes that laced up the front and came up over my ankles.

My mom would shake her head and tell me that I had never ridden on a train. I would tell her, completely exasperated, "I don't mean here! This was before, when I was eight years old!" Mind you, I was three or four when I was telling her this. I didn't know how to explain to her that I had ridden that train "back in my other life."

We lived in Hawaii at the time (my father was serving in the Coast Guard), and I think the event that may have triggered my recollection of the train ride was seeing a train set up for display on one of the old sugar cane plantations. Whatever triggered the recall, I still have the memory in my head . . . and I do remember it, vividly.

I was on my knees, facing the back of the seat, looking back at the other passengers and out the window, which was wide open due to the heat. Everything was covered in dust and soot. I was hot and sweaty. I wanted to take my bonnet off, but I wasn't allowed. I could smell the body odor of the people around me as well as the smell of burning coal. The scenery outside the window was mostly flat terrain, partially covered in scrub brush that was brown and dead looking for the most part.

Could it have been an invented memory from watching too many TV shows? I don't think so. Most TV shows back in the early 1960s tended to be antiseptic, in that they didn't really show the dirt, the sweat, and the smell. Is it really a memory from a former life? I think so. Maybe that also explains why I like old-fashioned things, and the old ways of doing things. If I had my way, I'd be homesteading up on some mountaintop right now, and to heck with electricity and running water!

—*Lori Howard Wolpert,*
Jeffersonville, Ind.

Beyond Déjà Vu

As logical and realistic as I am, I have always been extremely drawn toward studying the paranormal and the unknown. Through all my reading and researching over the years, I've found a lot of it to be darn convincing.

The experts say that we all dream every night, but I can rarely remember my dreams. Over the course of my lifetime I've had a few recurring dreams that I wake up remembering clearly. About four to six times per year I'll have this one dream in particular. Every time I have it, it's exactly the same. It has absolutely no relation to my life, which is what makes it so odd.

In real life, I'm a 30-year-old, all-American woman with blond hair and green eyes. But not in my dream. It always begins the same way. I am walking alongside slightly elevated train tracks. As I walk, I look down and see that I'm wearing worn, tattered, and stained work pants and filthy, muddy workboots. In one hand

I'm holding an old-fashioned black metal lunchbox, and I notice I have the arms and hands of a man. I never see my own face, but in the dream I know that I am a fairly young Mexican man, returning home from a long, hard day at work.

As I'm trudging along, I look over to my right and see one run-down home after the next. Some are makeshift huts constructed from mud, straw, and other scrap materials. I watch as a Mexican woman hangs clothes out to dry with a baby on her hip. I hear the clamor of people yelling and arguing, children screaming, and babies crying all around me. As I'm dragging myself home, a freight train comes blasting past on the tracks to my left, only adding to my irritation.

This dream is so vivid and clear, it's almost as if it's really happening. The young man's emotions are so strong, I can actually feel the hopelessness and depression. The overall feeling of melancholy overwhelms me. In the dream I know I live there. I live in poverty and I feel as though I will never be able to escape it. It's a feeling of total and utter despair.

That is where my dream ends, every time. But here's where my story gets weird.

In late August 2004, I made a trip to old Tijuana, Mexico, to have some dental work done. A few months earlier I had read an article about how stellar dentristry was in Mexico, for a fraction of U.S. prices. I was thrilled because I was in dire need of extensive work. So I began researching my options online. While I was searching I linked to a webpage containing lists of Mexican dentists. Curiously, I scrolled down the list and stopped at a name. Right then, I knew I had found my dentist; my search was over. His name just clicked with me and I felt good about him.

I called Dr. De La Vega on the phone and we spoke. I felt as though I knew him already. He knew exactly what I needed, with limited information from me.

I needed to have my whole mouth crowned, so I had to stay in Tijuana for about two weeks. I took my mother, Pamela Lamkin, and we flew to San Diego, then took a shuttle van to the hotel in the border town of San Ysidro, California.

As soon as we arrived in town, things got really eerie. I had never even been to California before, yet I knew instinctively where everything was. I even knew when our shuttle driver was going the wrong way and I had to redirect him to where we were staying. He was confused that I knew where everything was, but I had no explanation. This really creeped my mother out. She kept asking me, "How do you know?" over and over again.

The next morning we headed for the Mexican border on foot. I continued to know San Ysidro like the back of my hand. I could tell what was around every corner. But after we crossed the walking bridge to Tijuana, nothing seemed familiar.

I was already almost two hours late for my appointment at the dentist's office, so we quickly hailed a taxi. Unfortunately, I was delayed even longer because the taxi driver's English was worse than my Spanish. Eventually, he found the office, but he passed it by a couple of blocks. We told him to just drop us off where we were. I figured we were close enough.

As we were getting out of the taxi to unload our baggage, a man wearing a white coat came running down the street calling my name. My mother and I looked at each other in surprise. "How did he know it was us?" she asked me. I told her I had no idea; I never discussed my age or appearance with him.

When the dentist approached I asked him how he knew it was us. "I don't know; I just knew," he replied. Later, we discovered even more uncanny parallels. It was so weird because I felt like I had known him my whole life.

Two weeks later when he finished up all the work, we said our goodbyes and headed back to San Ysidro. We had tickets to fly back to Tampa that evening, but all the planes headed for Florida were grounded due to a hurricane. Upon finding this out, we found a room for the night at a different hotel.

Not long after checking in, I left my room on the third floor to seek out the vending machines. On my way back up, I stopped to look out over the balcony at the beautiful sunset. I heard a freight train coming as I was standing there. I looked down and I couldn't believe my eyes when it began to pass. The spot where I was standing was one of the few places that had a clear view of the railroad tracks along the outer limits of town. It immediately brought me back to another time, and I flashed back to my dream. All of a sudden, everything made sense. That was the spot I had been dreaming about. That was where I had lived as that Mexican man in a past life.

Finally, the mystery was solved and the loose ends tied up. I have not had the dream again.

—*Courtenay Savage,*
Spring Hill, Fla.

Little House in the Woods

When I was a very young girl I used to get into a cabinet that my mother kept empty for me because I insisted on having it. Once inside, with the door mostly closed, I would go away to my "Little House in the Woods." I don't know just how I went or came back, but I went there often.

The house itself was unpainted, lapstrake siding weathered gray. It was somewhere in the piney woods of East Texas, I believe. We lived in East Texas ourselves at that time and I never thought that the "little house" was too far away.

When I arrived at the little house, in whatever dream or visionary state I was in, it always seemed that

I really was there physically. I would be at the bottom of the front porch steps and would look around a little, enjoying the woods but vaguely wondering why the big pine trees grew so close; there was not much, if any yard. The weather was always the same when I went there, no matter the weather at my "real" house. At the little house it was not hot or cold. I never felt the temperature at all. Like the Little Bear's things in the story of Goldilocks, it was just right. Sunshine filtered down through the pine trees, dappling the ground, although the trees grew thickly enough that the whole area was mostly in shade.

After looking at my surroundings I would climb up the front steps and cross the small porch to the door. The door was closed but not locked, and I would open it and go inside. There was no furniture in the living room. I would sometimes wish that I had something to play with in the open expanse of floor. There was faded wallpaper on the walls, a pretty print with little bunches of pink flowers. It must have been cheery when it was new, but that had to have been long before. The house had the feel that it had not been inhabited in a long time. It was a well-made little house and did not have dust or other grime in it. I thought that the woman who had lived there had carefully swept and cleaned it before she left. I had the feeling that she had cherished that house and had not wanted to leave it dirty.

After looking around the living room I always went into the kitchen. It was a long narrow room in the back, right-hand corner. It had a counter that had been covered with linoleum. The linoleum had turned up on one corner. The cabinets under the counter were closed and I never looked into them. Across from the counter were a stove and a refrigerator. The stove was an old-fashioned one that stood on legs. Its white enamel matched the refrigerator. The refrigerator was the type that had a round compressor on top, though at that time I did not know what the round thing was. I called it a "refrigerator with a hat"!

After I looked briefly around I would go to the back door at the far end of the kitchen. Outside was a set of weathered wood steps that led down to the pine-needle-carpeted ground. I always marvelled that there was a very large pine tree just a couple of feet from the steps; I knew that it had grown there since the family had left. Pines in East Texas grow quickly; it could have grown there in about two decades, which would have meant that the family could have left at the end of the 1920s.

Strangely, though, I never went into the rest of the house; the bedrooms did not interest me, although I sensed that there were two of them and I always thought that the view from their windows was pretty.

My trip to the little house in the woods never varied. After I had gone to the back door and looked out, wary of the state of the old and crooked back steps that

I would not venture down, I would find myself back home in my beloved cabinet under the counter where our family's radio sat. I would listen to the late 1940s music awhile and then come out.

I wonder now if I had been the woman of that house. It was so familiar, and yet, without its furnishings, it was somehow devoid of emotion to me. But I liked it tremendously and I "went there" again and again.

—*Mary Holland Watson,*
Austin, Tex.

12

Spirit Guides and Angels

Cultures throughout time and across the globe have affirmed the existence of beings of a higher order, somewhere between human and divine. Known variously as angels, devas, bodhisattvas, or spirit guides, these benevolent intelligences are the teachers and protectors of humanity.

Encounters with such beings have been recorded from time immemorial and continue to the present day, as the following accounts attest.

Guardian Angel

David, my husband, had gone out of town to work, and sleep became a problem as irrational fear held me in a vise grip. I stayed awake all night listening for rattling doorknobs, footsteps on our deck, and tapping at our windows. It might have been the wind or my imagination, but to my senses it was a mass murderer on the other side. I left the lights on, pulled the covers over my head—anything to ease my anxiety.

My two children were as supportive as an eight- and eleven-year-old could be. We tried sleeping at different intervals so someone would always be awake to listen and watch in case someone broke in.

David's job would take five to six months; after three weeks I thought I'd be dead by the time he came home. My head hurt. My eyes stung. I felt like a zombie as I sleepwalked my way through each day. Life was miserable.

I knew in my heart that God would protect us. I had known and felt His protection before, but every night fear crept through the darkness and attached itself to me like a leech. Every night I prayed. Every morning, sometime around daybreak, I would fall asleep.

It was four days before Easter. The red numbers on the clock face mocked me as I placed my book on the nightstand. The clock read 3:43.

"Please, Lord," I prayed, "send someone to watch over us. I can't live like this anymore."

I told the kids good night, rolled over, and pulled the blanket up over my shoulders. Uncharacteristically, I fell asleep almost immediately.

"Michael," I said later, waking myself as I rolled over in bed. Opening my eyes, my gaze fell toward the door of the bedroom. I had left the hall light on. I glimpsed the back of a huge man floating out of the room. He was wearing a loose, white translucent robe.

"Who is it, Mom?" my daughter asked, sitting up on her floor pallet.

"Michael the archangel." The realization was so powerful, I didn't even question what I said.

"Probably so." She lay back down. I glanced back toward the doorway. A relaxing peace filled the room and I closed my eyes, falling back asleep. Later, when we woke up, we were rested.

I know some people don't believe me when I tell my story. They look at me as if I've grown another head. It may be hard for them to fathom, but I know what I felt and saw. And since that night, I've not been afraid.

—*Deborah Bouziden,*
Edmond, Okla.

The Call Compels the Answer

One very late night, I was returning from an evening class at Central YMCA College in Chicago when there was a blackout in the entire neighborhood. As I got off my bus, I could barely see a few feet ahead of me. To say I was frightened is putting it mildly.

I began walking toward our house, which was two blocks from the bus line, trembling and praying that nobody would jump out at me from behind the bushes. I was prompted to ask for help, and I very firmly spoke aloud: "Jesus, help me! I can't see where I'm going!"

I was taken aback by what happened next: About 15 feet in front of me there appeared three bright, orange-glowing lights, all different sizes from tennis-ball to bowling-ball size. They were suspended in midair and kept bouncing up and down in front of me, lighting the way.

To this day I cannot explain what they were or where they came from. I simply believe that if we "will" something strongly enough, a compatible surrounding life form (an energy, or your Guardian Angel) may respond. Words from the Bible went through my head, when Jesus said, "Knock and I shall answer." I believe that's what happened to me: the call compels the answer.

—*Ethel Rawson,*
Harwood Heights, Ill.

The Spirit Protectors

After almost 60 years on this Earth with a number of significant career positions behind me, including Chief of Police in a major police department, I find it ironic to be reporting a life experience that began when I was around two years old and continued until I was about 11.

During those tender years I had no idea why I was being thrust into the world of parapsychology but learned later that it was the result of my mother's health problems and feelings of desperation. When traditional medical science proved inadequate to deal with her physical and mental complaints, she and my father turned to a "faith healer" for help.

Sometime in early 1946, we drove into a suburb east of Baltimore City, Maryland, found the long driveway to the Traynor home, and parked behind the house. Mrs. Traynor was standing at the rear door inviting my parents to enter. My father mentioned the name of a co-worker who had referred them to her. Mrs. Traynor was probably in her late 60s, heavy with short-cropped hair. She had a motherly appearance and demeanor.

Inside the house, we were led to a large dining room and offered seats around a huge, old, wooden table. There were other people already there. The size of the group would vary, but usually numbered less than 20. Seated at the right end of the table was Mr.

Traynor. He was very frail and was usually slumped over in a rocking chair. He rarely spoke, and when he did he said very little.

Mrs. Traynor would escort one person at a time through a door leading off the dining room. When it was my turn to follow her through the door, I found myself standing in a small room facing a wall filled with lit candles in small red cups, such as you would see in a church. Although my memories have clouded somewhat over the years, I recall my fears changing to feelings of warmth and comfort when Mrs. Traynor turned to me and put her hand on my head. She then recited what I considered to be gibberish but was later explained to me as being a prayer spoken in German. Over the years, I would note the differences in her voice; sometimes her words were loud and emotional, sometimes soft, and sometimes she would even cry. When she was emotional, I would wonder what I had done wrong or what evil her words were warding off on my behalf.

After everyone had received their prayer, we would all take seats around the dining room table. Mr. Traynor would be turned to face the table and pulled close to it. As soon as the room was plunged into darkness, Mrs. Traynor would pray very softly and then summon her friendly "spirits" to join our gathering. Their arrival was very apparent, for they entered the body of Mr. Traynor and physically transformed him. The body of the frail, arthritic little man would straighten and he would display the appearance of a much younger and stronger man. Often their arrival was also signaled by a lifting or floating of the massive table.

Their voices were strong and youthful, and sounded to me just like those I'd heard in Western movies. Mrs. Traynor would assist with interpreting their messages. I recall being in awe of the transformation and no doubt at that early age somewhat frightened.

The spirits, we learned, were deceased American Indians. It was never clear how they connected with the Traynors, but I recall seeing pictures of the Traynors visiting Indians somewhere in what was said to be Oklahoma. Each of the spirits was identified by name. Blue Bird was the spirit who was the "protector of the children." My most vivid recollections are of those occasions when he would enter Mr. Traynor and speak to us. His voice was softer and less intimidating than some of the others; however, I remember having mixed emotions when he would come to us. I was eager to hear what he said, but I dreaded being singled out.

One evening when I was about ten years old, Blue Bird said my name rather abruptly and with obvious emotion and concern. He told me that some of my friends would ask me to get into a boat with them but that I should refuse. He said that if I went with them, I wouldn't come back. Talk about being scared!

About a week later I was playing down by the harbor in Baltimore with some of my buddies. One of them grabbed a small rowboat from a sand-and-gravel company and beached it where we were playing. My friends got into the boat and urged me to join them. With Blue Bird's warning fresh in my mind, I told them to go without me. When they were about 40 yards off shore, the boat capsized and one of the guys hit his head. He received a severe gash and lost consciousness. The other two were able to haul him to shore, which no doubt saved his life. I'm convinced to this day that had I ignored the warning, I'd have found my way to the bottom of the harbor.

On another occasion, Blue Bird called my name as we sat around the table and spoke in great detail about a situation I was experiencing in my neighborhood. A boy two years older and about 20 pounds heavier than me was bullying me and I felt compelled to fight with him twice in one week. I had lost both fights decisively and was at my wit's end. Although embarrassed to be singled out, I was excited to hear Blue Bird say that the problem would soon be no more.

A few days later, I met my problem face to face at the movie theater as I was going into the rest-room. When he saw me, his face filled with fear, and he almost fell over getting out of my way. He avoided me like the plague from then on. I actually felt sorry for him, and after a while I began to go out of my way to be friendly to him. I joined the Air Force when I was 17 and never saw him after that. I wish now I had asked him what happened to cause his change of attitude toward me, but I doubt that he would have been able to give me an accurate answer.

When newcomers would join the Traynors' group, the spirits would address them on their first evening and tell them personal things about themselves. These intimate revelations would astound and impress all of us and strengthen our faith in the Traynors and their spirits.

My parents told me that on their first visit, their spirit told them what they had for dinner that evening, a number of things about their parents, and described some of my mother's inner fears that brought her to the Traynors.

My parents felt privileged to have been led to the Traynors. They believed that the Traynors were doing God's work, if in a very nontraditional way. The Traynors were sincere, kindly, caring, and certainly not running some type of scam for money. My parents would give Mrs. Traynor five dollars sometimes; when things were tight, they didn't give her anything. To my knowledge, there was never a discussion of money, and whatever money people gave them was accepted graciously.

When I was about 11 years old, my mother "found Christ" at the Gospel Assembly church in Brooklyn. After receiving her salvation, she became convinced that the Traynor's work was of the devil and ceased all contact with them. I don't recall how much later my mother heard that Mr. Traynor had passed away and that Mrs. Traynor had sold the house. She would have been very old by then.

About 15 years ago, I drove by the old Traynor house, just to see it again and to give in to a curious urge to reminisce. The house had been renovated over the years, but was still standing. The neighborhood had changed dramatically, with houses where open spaces had been. I parked across from the house and watched three young children playing in the yard. As I watched, I saw what appeared to be an almost transparent image of an Indian warrior looking down over the children. My eyes were tearing somewhat, so maybe I didn't really see him. But then again, maybe I did.

—*Robert P. Russell,*
Gambrills, Md.

Voice in the Night

At 17, I was preparing for my high school graduation. My boyfriend of two years was getting ready to graduate from college. We were deeply in love and looked forward to a future together. When Bill proposed to me, I accepted with enthusiasm, babbling on about how my four years at college would probably pass quickly.

"You don't understand," Bill had said. "When we get married, you won't have to go to college. I'll take care of you."

Suddenly the future looked less bright. I tried to make him realize that college was important to me. But nothing I said helped him understand my position.

Finally, he gave me an ultimatum. "It's me or college. If you want to marry me, you must give up the idea of college. If you decide to go to college, then it's over between us. I'll call you tomorrow morning for your decision."

Tomorrow morning? How could I make such a choice by then? That night, as I tossed and turned in bed, sobbing uncontrollably, I repeatedly called out, "Oh God, what am I going to do?" I was not a religious person, but I was so distraught I didn't know where else to turn.

At some point in the night, I was awakened by a bright light flooding my bedroom. Thinking it was the sun and that I had overslept, I sat upright. Then a voice within me said, "Go to college." The light dimmed, and my bedroom was dark again. Calmness surged through me as I slid down under my covers. I knew what I would tell Bill the next day when he called.

In the morning, I asked my mother why she had come into my room in the middle of the night and turned on my light. She assured me that she hadn't been in my room at all. I related the event to her and we both agreed I had experienced something spiritual.

When Bill's call came, I told him calmly of my decision. The conversation was brief, and I never heard from him again.

—*Judy Wolfman,*
York, Pa.

To My Guardian Angel: Thanks

Most guardian angel stories are associated with children and not adults. My story also takes place in childhood, at age 12.

All my life I wanted a horse. I was the quintessential little girl who loved ponies, and after years of begging and promising to be good, my parents gave in. I got a horse.

Chief, my horse, was to live at my uncle's house in Eureka, Missouri, which was quite a few miles from my home. I didn't mind the drive except that the distance shortened my riding time. Because of this, I sometimes did not saddle Chief, choosing to ride bareback instead. It was on one of these short visits when my angel encounter occurred.

On this particular occasion, we were visiting for Thanksgiving dinner, as was the family tradition. All afternoon I had been riding bareback in the open field and now it was time to head for the trail. This trail was short, had a slight curve, and was approximately

40 yards long. My foster brother Gary, unbeknown to Chief and me, was in the woods.

Chief walked through the short trail and at the end, I turned him around to head back when all of a sudden—Crackle! Swoosh! Thump-thump!—Gary suddenly emerged from the brush at the trailhead, startling us both. I was a little surprised, but Chief was positively spooked. He reeled up slightly on his heels, pivoted 90 degrees on his hind legs, and darted off.

His sudden right-angle turn jarred me out of position. Chief broke into a gallop as I tried unsuccessfully to pull myself up. I found myself straddling my horse's belly, hanging on sideways for dear life. I was shell-shocked, frozen in a daze, knuckles white as snow as they squeezed, locked tight around his mane. I couldn't get myself back up.

"Let go."

Someone was speaking to me, not in the traditional sense but somehow communicating with me. I ignored him. I was too terrified. The voice repeated over and over, becoming more adamant.

"Let go. Let go. Let go!"

I was too frightened. I couldn't comprehend the words. As Chief galloped thunderously along, I looked up and saw the source of the message. There was the essence of my guardian angel. He was a brilliant white, his face framed by blondish brown hair. He hovered along with me just above Chief's back near my clenched hands. When he realized I wasn't going to let go, he reached over and released my grasp around Chief's mane. I fell to the ground.

I suffered a mild concussion from the fall, either from the impact of the ground or from Chief's back hoof. If my guardian angel hadn't released my grip, I would have been hurt far worse, as Chief picked up much more speed later on.

That is how I met my guardian angel. From that day on, I have believed in guardian angels, though I haven't seen him since.

—Mary Frey,
Mableton, Ga.

Guided by a Light

In July 1988, I was employed as a security officer for a gated community in Clermont, Florida, 35 miles from my home. My regular shift was from 3:00 to 11:00 p.m. I had to travel each day on Highway 27, which at the time was having work done along the shoulders, with a drop-off over one foot in places.

One day, the skies started clouding up around six or seven. By ten o'clock, lightning was flashing all around as far as I could see. My relief man showed up a few minutes after eleven, and as luck would have it, the rain started as I got in my car. Within 15 minutes, the rain was so fierce that I could not see but a few feet ahead of me. To make matters worse, water covered the road to a depth of several inches, so I did not dare pull off. I was probably as scared as I have ever been in my entire life. My hands were gripping the steering wheel as tightly as possible.

I finally cried out, "God! I am scared to death! I cannot see the road. Please help me get home safely."

Believe it or not, out of the pitch darkness a light appeared in the sky off to my left, about 200 yards ahead, illuminating the road in front of me. I still kept my speed down to about 15 miles per hour because the water was so deep. The light guided me all the way home, and disappeared as I pulled into my driveway. I sat there for several minutes as my body relaxed, and I thanked the Lord for bringing me home safely.

Many times in my life I have asked for help, and I have never been disappointed.

—*Daniel C. Tarry,*
Leesburg, Fla.

The End of the Road

It was June 2005, and we had planned the best family vacation ever: spending a week on the Big Island of Hawaii. While dreams of warm blue waters and glistening white sand beaches danced in mind, my 16-year-old son Paul looked forward to seeing waterfalls and an active volcano.

To appease my son, my husband Lawrence and I agreed that the first sight we visited would be the active volcano located at the Hawaii Volcanoes National Park, a trip that would take three to four hours. It was on the way to the Volcanoes National Park that our lives were put in potential danger and that my angels came to rescue us.

While traveling to the park, I noticed on the map that the Wind Farm was only half an hour off the road we were traveling on. I also noticed that the southern-most tip of the United States was only a few minutes farther south. We talked it over and agreed that the slight detour would not add too much extra time to our day; after all, we were supposed to be on vacation.

The Wind Farm, a man-made creation that harvests energy using the wind, is one of my favorite sights on the island. The sight of the windmills also raised the interest of my son, a budding photographer. After several great shots, we traveled south to the southern-most point of the United States.

On the way there we had breathtaking views of cliffs just to the right of us. The further south we drove, the clearer the vision of the cliffs became. Soon, we could spot the white tips of waves crashing upon the dark brown and black cliffs. The scene was enticing and we looked for a way to get closer so that we could get better photos.

Lawrence located a paved road off to the right and began to drive down the winding road closer and closer to the bottom of the cliffs. We grew very excited as we anticipated the magnificent views we would soon experience.

Suddenly, I heard the word "Stop!" shrieking in my head. It took me by surprise, and I could feel the adrenaline pumping into my body, which began to shake. Frantically, I screamed to my husband to stop the car. I told him that I had to get out of the car and walk the rest of the way down.

Lawrence looked at me, puzzled and unsure what to do. When I repeated my request to stop, he did so.

I quickly got out of the car, not knowing why I had to walk the rest of the way on foot. Paul decided he would get out too, and we both started to walk down the rest of the way. Perhaps it was something in my demeanor, but Lawrence put the car in park right there in the middle of the road, got out, and followed us.

As we made the turn around the bend in the road, which was only about 20 feet in front of our parked car, we all stood there, frozen and shocked. Then we looked at each other in utter disbelief. The rest of the road had crumbled away. Large chunks of pavement lay scattered over the rocks below, a good 60-foot drop.

No one knew when the road had crumpled; maybe it was from one of the earthquakes that wrack the island from time to time, or it could have been a simple erosion problem. But whatever the reason, there were no warning signs or any other hints that the road had collapsed into the ocean.

We took the pictures that we had risked our lives to get and headed back up the road. On our way up the road we met several other tourists who were making their way down the winding road to the bottom of the cliff.

When we told them about our experience, they were astounded and thanked us profusely.

Everyone thanked my angels for being there to protect us that day.

—*Francine Milford,*
Venice, Fla.

Angel by My Side

On a late afternoon in the early spring of 1972 I was involved in my second auto accident in ten months. Another drunk driver hit my car, but this time the injuries were devastating. I blacked out for a moment. When coming to I witnessed the smoldering wreckage of the other vehicle. For sure I thought the other driver was dead. Twisted metal blocked my view for a moment. *Don't panic*, I thought. *Someone will come to help you.* But it seemed forever before anyone arrived.

I couldn't move my legs. Then the pain became unbearable. My chest felt crushed and it became difficult to take air into my lungs. The next thing I remember was being taken on a stretcher into Midland Memorial, the closest hospital in the area. Within minutes a group of doctors were standing over me.

"You're badly injured," the doctors said as they began pumping painkillers into my arm. Within seconds I was asleep.

Late that night I awoke to a night nurse by my side. She appeared young, yet compassionate.

"How are you feeling?" she asked in a quiet tone of voice.

My eyes were blurry and the nurse faded in and out of sight. "What time is it?" I asked.

"It's three a.m." she replied. Then she touched my arm.

Her hand felt hot, but I did not pull my arm away. I kept drifting in and out of sleep for the rest of the night. Yet each time I woke I could see the young nurse standing by my side. By dawn she was gone.

The second night she lifted me up so that I could sit by the edge of my bed. It was three in the morning again and she would stay till dawn each night. I thought it was unusual that a night nurse would spend several hours with one patient.

"What is your name?" I asked.

"Selva," she replied.

Unusual name, I thought. It didn't matter. Selva was an angel to me. She took the time to spend a few hours with a helpless person and I thought it to be a great act of kindness.

On the third night she came into my room again. It was three o'clock.

"You are being moved tomorrow to another hospital," she said. "I won't be seeing you again. I cannot stay with you very long this night; so much work to do."

Selva touched my hand. Her touch was very warm, but again had no burning effect. I must have fallen off to sleep.

When I woke, Selva was gone. I felt an emptiness I had never experienced before. I just wanted to see her one last time. What a beautiful nurse to take so much time out for me!

The next morning they came to move me to Copper Hospital, a place where they would be better equipped to heal my legs. The pain seemed to subside. This was strange even with painkillers.

On the way through the hallway, I asked to stop at the main floor desk. I had a note for Selva that I wanted her to have in gratitude of all she done. I handed it to the head nurse.

"Give this to Selva," I requested.

The nurse looked at me in a serious manner. "Who is Selva?" she asked.

"The night nurse."

"Sir, there is no night nurse working here named Selva."

"What are you talking about? She came to my room every night about three in the morning."

"I would know her," the head nurse explained. "I know everyone that's on this floor."

I spent another few weeks in Copper Hospital. After being discharged I visited Midland a few more times, searching for Selva. Perhaps she was an illusion from the heavy medication I was on at the time. Or was she something else?

—*Dennis Ambrose,*
Vineland, N.J.

The Voice

As a young girl of approximately 14 years of age, I didn't have any experience with alcohol. My family were not drinkers; in fact, I never saw my mom take a drink of alcohol. My parents kept liquor and drink mixes in the house strictly for guests, and these were stored in a kitchen cabinet high over the stove.

Late one evening, while my mom and brother were asleep in their beds and my dad was on duty at the fire station where he worked as a fire chief, I sat by myself in our living room reading a book to make myself sleepy enough to go to bed. As I was reading I got an overwhelming craving for a bloody mary. My mouth was even watering in anticipation of the drink. Now, as I said, up to that point in my life I had never had any liquor, let alone a bloody mary, so I was bewildered as to where such a craving could have come from.

The craving was getting stronger so I went into the kitchen, stood on a small step stool, and opened the liquor cabinet. I saw a bartender's book and looked up bloody mary instructions. It looked simple enough to make, so I took down the vodka bottle. Behind it was a bottle of bloody mary mix. Even easier, I thought.

I got a juice glass and proceeded to mix what tasted to my untrained taste buds like the perfect bloody mary. We didn't have any celery stalks like the drink book called for, but that was okay. I took my drink back into the living room and proceeded to sip and read.

I had just taken another sip and was feeling very grown up and worldly when a voice outside my left ear said my full name.

"Judith Marie!"

It sounded like an angry parent scolding a child. I froze, staring at the page of my book, not wanting to believe what I had just heard. I knew it wasn't either of my parents' voices I had just heard, so I convinced myself that I hadn't heard anything and went back to reading. Then the voice said my name again.

"Judith Marie!"

This time my heart felt like it stopped beating and my breath caught in my throat, but I forced myself to look in the direction of where I heard the voice, afraid of what I might see or not see. With false teenage courage (and the drink didn't hurt), I spoke back to the unseen voice: "What?"

There was no one standing there, and the voice didn't answer me back, but I somehow knew that it was admonishing me for drinking and wanted me to throw the rest of the drink away. Shaken, I got up and went back to the kitchen. I threw the drink in the sink and washed the glass. Then I went to bed.

This happened in the mid-1970s. In 2004 I had my first psychic reading and the psychic told me that the voice I heard as a teen had been my spirit guide, Patricia. I'd like to say that hearing a disembodied voice as a young person scared me so badly that I never touched alcohol again, but it didn't. Again in my teens, but a few years after that incident, I had a near-death experience from alcohol poisoning and ended up in the emergency room for 38 hours. Most of that time was spent in an alcohol-induced coma.

That experience is what put the stopper in the bottle for me. I haven't touched alcohol since. Thanks, Patricia!

—*Judith Stemen,*
Bloomington, Calif.

Birch Dreams

I turned 12 in the summer of 1972, and I would remember this year for the rest of my life as a magical age. We had recently moved from the city to a place called Pine Hills near the small town of Julian, California. I'd always been somewhat of a loner but was even more so now that we lived in the mountains surrounded by old oaks and tall pine trees.

Not long before our move (in fact, our move had been precipitated by this event), I had a series of disturbing clairvoyant dreams of seeing myself chased by a mob of kids. This vision played out in real life, and I was still recovering from the event, confused and disillusioned. I was untrusting and unwilling to make new friends. Instead, I spent my time alone in the woods.

Trees were easy to be with. From an early age I had been a tree person, making herbal poultices for the injured trees on our property and often just climbing up to sit in one for long periods of time. Now that I had hills of trees to explore and enjoy, I did so at every opportunity. I was lulled to sleep by the peaceful lullaby of the wind whistling through the tree tops.

That summer I began to have another series of unusual dreams, but this time they were comforting. They lasted for nearly a year, and they always began and ended exactly the same way. I would be walking in the forest, admiring the trees as I walked, and everything would become extremely vivid. Subtle colors and textures stood out along with the natural sounds and smells of the forest. I could even feel the breeze on my skin.

I would stop to gaze upon a particular tree when suddenly a loud rustling of leaves would cause me to turn and look away. As soon as I turned my head back around, a man appeared where there had been a tree before. We'd move along through the forest, sometimes slowly and sometimes quickly, as if gliding along somehow. Our conversations were often deep and inspiring but I also remember exhilarating feelings of pure joy, unlike anything I could formerly imagine. At some point I would hear or feel the gust again and turn my head away for a moment. When I looked back for him, there would only be trees in the forest again. The happy feelings lingered after I woke up, even though the context was already lost.

My healing occurred between these two head-turning points. From the first time I had this dream, I felt inexplicably drawn to the man in my dream. This was completely out of line with my personality. I immediately trusted and loved him for some unknown reason. He felt more familiar to me than anyone I'd ever actually known. He told me his name was Birch. Birch trees didn't grow in that area, or if they did, I was not aware of it, but that's what he told me his name was. He referred to the pines and oaks as the "friends," and that much I could understand.

The gist of our conversation seemed to involve issues that concerned me in my waking life. The feeling I had when seeing Birch was like getting together with a trusted and beloved friend, and the communication was effortless. The remnants of hurt and betrayal in my waking life vanished in his presence. His way of speaking was so unpredictable that I would see things in an entirely different way than before. It was absolutely judgment-free, neither agreeing nor disagreeing with my depictions of events. He helped me shift to a different point of view. It was as if some greater part of me was aware, even if the usual intellectual processes of thinking and recall seemed off.

Birch listened to my emotional renditions of reality, just like a friend would do, and he would gently call attention to some aspect of the natural world in response: an injured bird, the way a flower was growing, or the changing appearance of the slanting light through the trees. At some point I would understand the significance and it would feel like, "ah-ha!" This seemed to bring on the gust and the head-turning and his disappearance.

Waking up in my bed I would have the very real sensation of just having been outside in the forest with Birch. It was as though I didn't sleep for a year, and I didn't have any other dreams during this time either. But I always felt a deep sense of peace and happiness upon waking. The curious thing was, I made many attempts to recall his appearance, thinking I would like to draw a picture of him, but I never could remember even the slightest thing about how he looked. My feelings, however, told me he was indescribably beautiful. I also made attempts over the year to record his exact words to me, with the same result. There was only the immeasurable sense of blessedness. I knew I would find him again the next night anyway. I came to rely upon it. In fact, I came to rely upon Birch to the exclusion of all else. I was no longer sad and confused, just anxious to sleep so I could meet him again.

Then one night Birch told me something I remembered. He said we would no longer be meeting like this. I laughed when I woke up because I knew I could dream him as I'd been doing, maybe forever. I was crushed when the dreams really did cease. More desperately than ever I tried to recall his words. I kept trying to picture Birch, thinking if I could recall his appearance I could locate him.

In spite of all my efforts, the nights became ordinary again, and I could not dream him back. I have not dreamed of him since. All I had left were deep impressions of gratitude and love.

I felt truly heartbroken, as if I'd lost the greatest friend and love of my life. He would have been the one I confided in so I dealt with it alone. I looked for him in both dreams and real life for many years. But now I know he was only mine for a time, a time when I needed his healing.

Shortly after the dreams ended, I began making friends again and my longing slowly gave way to moments of wistful daydreams. I made the transition into my teenage years with more compassion than anger, and a sense of awe instead of disillusionment when I looked at the world.

I still don't know how these dreams came about, or the origin of Birch. If he was only a dream, what a beautiful dream I had for a year. I sometimes wonder if some child somewhere is talking and walking with Birch now. I hope it's true.

—*Jeannie Beck,*
Borrego Springs, Calif.

The Tenth-of-a-Second Detour

It was snowing lightly that night in May 1994 when I turned my pickup onto the road and headed down the mountain.

Closing the bar had been a breeze; the crowd dissipated, and the regulars had all left early. Spring weather made snow conditions less than ideal for most skiers; they complained of ice in the morning and slush in the afternoon, along with sunburns and sticking skis. Soon there wouldn't be any snow at all, and that was fine by me. It had been a good season in the resort town of Brian Head, Utah.

Ernie was the last customer to leave the bar. He stopped by to drop off a fine bottle of wine, already corked, before driving to the Vegas airport. We had a toast to the end of a long, cold winter. I didn't think anything of it when I tucked the bottle behind the seat of my pickup and strapped myself in.

"Drat!" I cussed as I took the seat belt off. I had forgotten to turn my hubs in; there had to be ice under that new-fallen snow, and being in four-wheel drive made me feel a whole lot safer.

A clean white field of snow stretched from the forest on one side of the road to the forest on the other side. There was no way to tell where the edges of the road were except for the tiny reflectors placed every hundred yards or so along the right side of the highway. It was obvious no one had been up or down for some time.

My headlights reflected off the ice crystals clinging to the limbs of the aspens. A heavy snow load weighed down the branches of the spruce and pines from the last storm, now passing away.

There wouldn't be any plow up at this time of night, I reminded myself. The standard procedure is to take it really easy, especially in the turns—and that's mostly all there is until reaching the valley.

I breathed a sigh of relief when the road leveled out and entered the small town at the foot of the mountain. The treacherous part of the journey home was over, although a light snow was still gently drifting to the ground.

This called for a toast to the snow gods for a safe ride to a warm bed. I reached behind the seat, pulled the cork, and took a long draught from the wine bottle.

The short ride through town to the interstate gave me no confidence in better driving conditions. Gently using the brakes confirmed the presence of ice as one wheel or another momentarily locked up. This was the stuff no one wants to drive on, ominously called "black ice."

Nonetheless, the warmth in my gut felt good as I uncorked the bottle again and took another healthy swig. Time to turn the music up as a Yanni tape began turning on its spindles.

Odd, I thought, as my trusty Toyota headed down the on-ramp to the interstate—there were absolutely no other cars in sight.

The highway ran straight and true, and gave me a sense of safety, unlike the curvy mountain roads. I settled on a speed that seemed safe. As long as I didn't need to turn my wheel, there wasn't any danger of sliding. Or so I thought.

It came unexpectedly. My pickup began a slow slide away from the straight and narrow. My wheels had no traction. There was not the slightest hint of any slowing; my vehicle continued to veer to the left. Fortunately, my momentum continued sending me straight down the highway. An experienced winter driver, I slowly and carefully turned my wheels into the skid, attempting to correct for the position of my truck.

A wave of relief washed over me as the nose began turning back to the center. But it was short-lived; now a new terror confronted me. Though I had come back to a straightforward position, the truck continued turning in the other direction. I was in big trouble. While my momentum had been sending me straight down the highway before, I was now sliding toward the edge of the road. I looked out my left window and knew that when my wheels hit the side of the road I would roll over, and the driver's side would hit the ground first.

Then a very strange thing happened. My vision began to darken, almost like a veil being drawn over my eyes. What was happening?

The next thing I knew was total confusion. I seemed to be out of my truck walking around. There were two images, like a double exposure on film, and no way of telling which set was real. My truck, with me at the wheel, appeared suspended about six feet above the ground and inclined at a weird angle, frozen in time. The image was not solid, but rather like a vision or a dream. What the heck was going on?

My side of this double image didn't leave much room to see around; it was hazy and limited in scope, and very little could be made out to understand my predicament. What to do?

Wait! Did I see someone? How could that be? Yes, in the mist, someone was doing something. I felt fear and relief at the same time. This was all too eerie, but maybe I could get some answers.

I cautiously approached what appeared to be a figure taking notes. He turned abruptly as I approached and a smile came across his face.

"There you are," he said.

"What the hell is going on?" I asked.

He chuckled a little. "My name's Jake; we're here to try and fix this mess."

I felt immediately at ease, and suddenly very curious. "Uh, yeah, I think that's a really good idea, but I'm totally mixed up."

Through the haze in the background, there appeared to be other figures moving around. The central image was my truck, with me inside wearing a horrified look. But it just didn't seem real because I could virtually see through everything.

"Yes, these are unusual circumstances, and it doesn't happen very often, but when it does we certainly understand how you feel."

I hesitated a little and asked, "I wonder if you might help me figure out what this is all about?"

"Sure," he said. "Come over here and sit a minute."

I felt very relieved and more relaxed; someone was in charge here, and my confidence began to return.

"It's really quite simple; you're about to die in just a few more seconds. Problem is, it's not your time to die. That's what I and my crew do; we're fixer-uppers when things get out of whack."

"Oh dear, can you fix this mess?"

Jake looked up at my truck and pondered a second or two. "Well, in your situation, it's a little more complicated because we have to alter the laws that govern the physical world. When that's the case, we have to get okays from the highest authorities; normally it's forbidden.

I paused. "I had a feeling that it was all over for me the last time I looked out the window; just like what I'm doing in the truck right now. Can you tell me more about how you're going to work this out?"

"When it became obvious your survival was at a high level of doubt, an injunction came through that in effect suspended time for about a tenth of a second. We're in that window of time right now, and since the dimension we're in happens to exist outside the bounds of physical laws, we can go about our business setting new conditions in the other dimension that will, hopefully, get you back on track with your life. See?"

"Well, I can only say that I thank you very much; nothing could sound better than that. I'm not only awed, but humbled to think that such efforts are worth saving my life. Is this happening because I'm special or something like that?"

Jake looked down at his notebook, and then at my truck suspended in midair at a slightly odd angle.

"Yes, you are, but then so is everyone else. Life is special here on this planet, and human life especially. You have a meaning and purpose for being here; I can't tell you what that is because I don't know, but everything is done to help you and others from this side of reality, within the limits set for us. That's part of our purpose for being here too. Every person has the potential to do wondrous things; improving conditions in the world is high on the list, but only time will tell whether they attain their goals or not. Those goals are unique to the individual; no two people have identical roles to play in life, just as my role here is to fix problems dealing with time and space, while others help travelers adjust from one dimension to another. Does that make sense?"

I nodded, and thought about what Jake had said as he got up and hailed one of his crew. I existed and was as real as ever, but my body—totally undisturbed at the moment—was in another place. I'd read of strange stories like this, and wondered if I was now experiencing my own. Many people scoffed at the idea of life after death. Was this proof? I didn't know anything for sure, but I was still a conscious, thinking being lost somewhere between dimensions or worlds or time niches or mental states or who knows what.

I looked up as Jake approached. Behind him, my truck now appeared perfectly normal.

"Well, John, we're about done here. Our time warp is going to close soon. You'll be back almost to the moment you left your truck. You should be able to handle things from that point on."

"Wait, Jake," I almost shouted. "There's so much I'd like to talk to you about. Do we have to part so soon?"

"Can't help it; we dare not let this time gap stretch any wider, or things could get beyond our control. That we can do this at all is the real miracle; I guess it's what's called progress on this side of the spectrum. Take care. We'll meet again, in another time and place; until then, goodbye."

It seemed like a veil was lifted away from my eyes. I was still sliding, but now I was going straight down the highway. Much of my momentum had been lost as my truck made one final half-spin and came to rest on the shoulder of the road facing the direction I had just come from.

Several miles down the interstate I pulled off into a truck stop, parked, got out, and walked around my truck several times. I thought long and hard about what had just happened, then reached behind the seat, pulled the wine bottle out and dropped it into a trash barrel. I knew the wine wasn't an issue, but had there been a wreck, it wouldn't have looked good.

Had I been rescued from an ignoble death, and given another chance to live out my life? Jake didn't know my destiny any more than he knew anyone else's. Who are the higher authorities? Jake never mentioned religion, or used any terms like God.

I had no doubt that I had almost skidded off the road, but did that tenth-of-a-second detour really happen? I'll always wonder.

—*John Hammelton,*
Flagstaff, Ariz.

Angel of Death

On a wintry morning in December 2001, I stood alone in the window of an old flower shop where I worked as a designer, watching the lake-effect snow circle the building. The city street seemed deserted but for a black hearse creeping through the storm to the garage entrance of the funeral parlor next door.

I'd just finished the flowers for another afternoon wake, and the scent of chrysanthemums permeated my hair, a reminder of the sympathy tributes I often wore home each day.

St. John Kanty's, a grand gothic church, loomed across the street, ringing out a melody of hymns. When the doors opened, a small crowd quietly exited. Pallbearers in pristine white gloves heaved the casket into a silver hearse. The people scattered into red-flagged cars and slowly filed into a solemn procession.

As I blessed their departure, a dark figure drifted from the church, as if it was measuring my emotion. Faceless and ethereal, he walked through the snow without footprints, erasing the trace of his breath blowing in a shadow from beneath a low-brimmed fedora.

I'd seen him before. The room was dim in a fluorescent glow of illness at the bedside of last rites. His welcome presence twinkled in my mind's eye: there beside my mother, Lauretta Petkowicz, so many years ago. In a childish cry, I shed tears of gratitude even though I feared my own fate. She was finally free from pain, lifeless in the arms of an angel, soaring in the light of his love.

My fateful friend, this Angel of Death, crossed the street and followed the black hearse into the garage on the heels of the mortician. The door sealed them inside and the snow quickly frosted any remnant of the phenomenon.

I wondered why my vision had captured his image again. Why was I so privileged? Perhaps to tell you that his presence isn't grim. This Dark Angel is a being of grace whose purpose is comfort when transition can be chaos, the gentle guide who bears the souls of the willing homeward.

—*Khimm Graham,*
Buffalo, N.Y.

GET MORE AT LLEWELLYN.COM

Visit us online to browse hundreds of our books and decks, plus sign up to receive our e-newsletters and exclusive online offers.

- **Free tarot readings • Spell-a-Day • Moon phases**
- **Recipes, spells, and tips • Blogs • Encyclopedia**
- **Author interviews, articles, and upcoming events**

GET SOCIAL WITH LLEWELLYN

Find us on
Facebook
www.Facebook.com/LlewellynBooks

Follow us on
twitter
www.Twitter.com/Llewellynbooks

GET BOOKS AT LLEWELLYN

LLEWELLYN ORDERING INFORMATION

Order online: Visit our website at www.llewellyn.com to select your books and place an order on our secure server.

Order by phone:
- Call toll free within the U.S. at 1-877-NEW-WRLD (1-877-639-9753)
- Call toll free within Canada at 1-866-NEW-WRLD (1-866-639-9753)
- We accept VISA, MasterCard, and American Express

Order by mail:
Send the full price of your order (MN residents add 6.875% sales tax) in U.S. funds, plus postage and handling to: Llewellyn Worldwide, 2143 Wooddale Drive Woodbury, MN 55125-2989

POSTAGE AND HANDLING

STANDARD (U.S. & Canada):
(Please allow 12 business days)
$25.00 and under, add $4.00.
$25.01 and over, FREE SHIPPING.

INTERNATIONAL ORDERS (airmail only):
$16.00 for one book, plus $3.00 for each additional book.

Visit us online for more shipping options. Prices subject to change.

FREE CATALOG!

To order, call
1-877-
NEW-WRLD
ext. 8236
or visit our
website